◆ ◆ ◆ ◆ ◆ ◆ ◆

ERNST & YOUNG'S GUIDE TO THE NEW TAX LAW

Ernst & Young

John Wiley & Sons, Inc.

New York • Chichester • Brisbane • Toronto • Singapore

In the preparation of this book, every effort has been made to offer the most current, correct, and clearly expressed information possible. Nonetheless, inadvertant errors can occur and tax rules and regulations often change.

Further, the information in the text is intended to afford general guidelines on matters of interest to taxpayers. The application and impact of tax laws can vary widely from case to case, however, based upon the specific or unique facts involved. Accordingly, the information in this book is not intended to serve as legal, accounting, or tax advice. Readers are encouraged to consult with professional advisors for advice concerning specific matters before making any decision, and the author and publishers disclaim any responsibility for positions taken by taxpayers in their individual cases or for any misunderstanding on the part of readers. The information included in this book is based on the *Omnibus Budget Reconciliation Act of 1993* (Public Law 103–66), signed into law August 10, 1993.

◆ ◆ ◆ ◆ ◆ ◆ ◆
CONTENTS

Special Table of Contents by Industry   *vii*

Introduction   *x*

Overview of Major Tax Changes   *xiii*

The Economic Impact of the Act: Questions & Answers   *xxxi*

Table of Effective Dates   *xliii*

1. **Changes of Concern to Individuals   1**

    Regular Tax Rate Increases and Capital Gains Rate   **1**

    Tax Planning in Response to Higher Tax Rates   **4**

    Phase-out of Personal Exemptions   **12**

    Limitation on Itemized Deductions   **14**

    Taxation of Social Security Benefits   **16**

    Earned Income Tax Credit   **19**

    Medicare Tax Increase   **23**

    Estimated Taxes   **25**

    Alternative Minimum Tax   **28**

    AMT Exemption for Gifts of Appreciated Property   **32**

    Substantiation Requirements for Charitable Contributions   **35**

    Estate and Gift Tax Rates   **38**

    Repeal of Luxury Excise Tax on Boats, Aircraft, Jewelry, and Furs   **40**

Health Insurance Deduction for Self-Employed
Individuals   **42**

Capital Gains Incentive for Investment in Small
Business   **43**

Rollover of Gain From Sale of Publicly Traded
Securities Into Specialized Small Business
Investment Companies   **48**

**2. Changes of Concern to Business in
General   51**

Corporate Tax Rates   **51**

Accumulated Earnings and Personal Holding Company
Taxes   **55**

Corporate Estimated Taxes   **57**

Alternative Minimum Tax Relief   **61**

Moving Expense Deduction   **63**

Business Meals and Entertainment   **65**

Employer Tax Credit for FICA Taxes on Tip
Income   **66**

Club Dues   **68**

Lobbying Expense Deduction   **70**

Travel Expenses for Spouses, Dependents, and Other
Individuals   **74**

Extension of Research and Development Credit   **76**

Small Business Equipment Expensing Election   **78**

Withholding Rate on Supplemental Wages   **79**

Empowerment Zones and Enterprise
Communities   **80**

Amortization of Goodwill and Other Intangible
Assets   **89**

Repeal of Stock-for-Debt Exception   **100**

Expansion of Tax Attributes Reduced by Cancellation
of Indebtedness   **102**

State and Local Business Tax Considerations   **106**

3. Compensation and Benefits Changes   110

Employer-Provided Educational Assistance   **110**

Extension of Targeted Jobs Tax Credit   **112**

Reduced Compensation for Qualified Retirement Plan Purposes   **113**

Executive Compensation—Deduction Limitations   **117**

4. Provisions Affecting the Financial Services Industry and Investment Interests   121

Mark to Market for Securities Dealers' Inventories   **121**

Federal Assistance Payments Made to Certain Thrifts   **129**

Limitation on Use of Capital Gain Generators and Other Conversion Techniques   **131**

5. Provisions Affecting Real Estate   140

Low-Income Rental Housing Tax Credit   **141**

Mortgage Revenue Bonds   **142**

Passive Activity Loss Liberalization   **143**

Pension Fund and Other Investments in Real Estate   **149**

Discharge of Real Property Business Indebtedness   **153**

Partnership Redemptions   **158**

Depreciation of Nonresidential Real Property   **162**

6. Provisions Affecting Multinational Corporations   164

Transfer Pricing Compliance   **164**

Allocation of R&E Expenses   **168**

Deferral of Tax on Foreign Earnings and Changes to the Passive Foreign Investment Company Regime   **170**

Other Modifications to Subpart F/Same Country Exception **176**

Modification to the Investment of Earnings in U.S. Property Rule **177**

Possession Tax Credit **178**

Earnings Stripping and Other Anti-Avoidance Rules **182**

Foreign Tax Credit for Oil Multinationals **186**

7. Energy Taxes 189

Transportation Fuels Tax **189**

Collection of Diesel Fuel Excise Tax **191**

Extension of Motor Fuels Excise Tax **192**

Imposition of Excise Tax on Diesel Fuel Used in Noncommercial Motorboats **193**

8. Compliance 195

Expansion of 45-Day Interest-Free Period for Refunds **195**

Information Reporting (Discharge of Indebtedness) **197**

Increased Standard for Accuracy-Related and Preparer Penalties **199**

9. Miscellaneous Items 202

Index **204**

◆ ◆ ◆ ◆ ◆ ◆ ◆

SPECIAL TABLE OF CONTENTS BY INDUSTRY

For the convenience of those readers who are interested in how and to what extent a specific industry has been affected by the tax act, we have prepared these content listings on an industry-specific basis. This special table of contents contains those items (other than rate changes, estimated taxes, executive compensation limits, etc., which affect all taxpayers) that we believe may have a significant effect on a particular industry.

Financial Services Industry

"Mark to Market" for Securities Dealers' Inventories   **121**

Federal Assistance Payments Made to Certain Thrifts   **129**

Limitation on Use of Capital Gain Generators and Other Conversion Techniques   **131**

Rollover of Gain From Sale of Publicly Traded Securities Into Specialized Small Business Investment Companies   **48**

Repeal of Stock-for-Debt Exception   **102**

Expansion of Tax Attributes Reduced by Cancellation of Indebtedness   **100**

Information Reporting (Discharge of Indebtedness)   **197**

Amortization of Goodwill and Other Intangibles   **89**

Employer-Provided Educational Assistance **110**

Lobbying Expense Deduction **70**

Low-Income Rental Housing Tax Credit **40**

Health Care Industry

Employer-Provided Educational Assistance **110**

Amortization of Goodwill and Other Intangible
    Assets **89**

Depreciation of Nonresidential Real Property **162**

See also "Not-for-Profit Organizations"

Manufacturing/High Technology

Alternative Minimum Tax Relief (Corporations) **61**

Lobbying Expense Deduction **70**

Extension of Research and Development Credit **76**

Employer-Provided Educational Assistance **110**

Transfer Pricing Compliance **164**

Allocation of R&E Expenses **168**

Deferral of Tax on Foreign Earnings and Changes to the
    Passive Foreign Investment Company
    Regime **170**

Low-Income Rental Housing Tax Credit **141**

Depreciation of Nonresidential Real Property **162**

Orphan Drug Tax Credit **202**

Not-For-Profit Organizations

AMT Exemption for Gifts of Appreciated
    Property **32**

Substantiation Requirements for Charitable
    Contributions **35**

Employer-Provided Educational Assistance **110**

Lobbying Expense Deduction **70**

Pension Fund and Other Investments in Real
    Estate **149**

Depreciation of Nonresidential Real Property   **162**

Real Estate

Mortgage Revenue Bonds   **142**

Low-Income Rental Housing Tax Credit   **141**

Passive Activity Loss Liberalization   **143**

Pension Fund and Other Investments in Real Estate   **149**

Depreciation of Nonresidential Real Property   **162**

Discharge of Real Property Business Indebtedness   **153**

Expansion of Tax Attributes Reduced by Cancellation of Indebtedness   **100**

Partnership Redemptions   **158**

Information Reporting (Discharge of Indebtedness)   **197**

Retail

AMT Exemption for Gifts of Appreciated Property   **32**

Extension of Targeted Jobs Tax Credit   **112**

Repeal of Luxury Excise Tax on Boats, Aircraft, Jewelry and Furs   **40**

Depreciation of Nonresidential Real Property   **162**

Extension of Motor Fuels Excise Tax   **192**

Transportation Fuels Tax   **189**

Collection of Diesel Fuel Excise Tax   **191**

Lobbying Expense Deduction   **70**

Transfer Pricing Compliance   **164**

Amortization of Goodwill and Other Intangibles   **89**

Alternative Minimum Tax Relief   **61**

Small Business Equipment Expensing Election   **78**

◆ ◆ ◆ ◆ ◆ ◆ ◆
INTRODUCTION

How will the just-passed Omnibus Budget Reconciliation Act of 1993 affect your tax bill? The short answer is,
"It depends." Most low-income taxpayers will experi-
ence little change; all taxpayers will have some (usually
minor) impact due to higher gasoline taxes; but those in
the upper income group will feel a real jolt. For example,
the new 36% tax rate will apply to you if your *taxable
income* (your total income less deductions) exceeds
$140,000 for married couples (or $115,000 for a single
individual). Further, the new 10% surtax applies if your
taxable income (exclusive of capital gains) exceeds
$250,000. If you are affected, moreover, one of the most
onerous aspects of these new rates is that they are *retroactive to January 1, 1993.*

Who else will pay more taxes?

- Anyone with salary and wages of more than $135,000
  will pay in 1994 the 1.45% Medicare tax on *all* such
  earned income. For example, if your total wages are
  $180,000, your Medicare tax will rise from $1,958 to
  $2,610. And if you are self-employed, such as a
  partner in a law firm or a consultant, your Medicare
  tax will rise even further since self-employed persons pay at a 2.9% rate.

- Social Security recipients with other sources of
  income may also see their tax bill rise in 1994 if their
  income exceeds $44,000 for a married couple or
  $34,000 for an unmarried individual.

- Self-employed individuals and all businesses will see many of their business deductions cut back or eliminated in 1994. For example, the expenses for business meals will only be 50% deductible; the business deduction for social club dues (such as those paid to a country club) will be eliminated; and the costs you incur for your spouse's travel expenses accompanying you on a business trip will generally be disallowed unless your spouse's presence has a bona fide business purpose and he or she is an employee of the business bearing the cost.

In any tax bill, there are winners as well as losers. The Omnibus Budget Reconciliation Act of 1993 (the Act) provides relief to real estate professionals who formerly were unable to deduct their economic losses from their other sources of taxable income. It also relaxes a rule that put a damper on contributions of appreciated property to museums and other charitable institutions. In addition, the new law provides you the opportunity to invest in certain types of start-up ventures and potentially reap a sizable tax benefit if you sell your appreciated stock in the venture after holding it at least five years.

If you are affected by the new higher tax rates, there are tax-planning strategies you can implement to minimize the impact. The new law will prompt some taxpayers to escape tax through investments in such vehicles as municipal bonds and funds. Higher tax rates also enhance the benefits of deferred compensation plans, such as 401(k) plans and Keogh plans, as well as life insurance policies that offer tax-free inside build-up. Further, with the differential between the maximum statutory capital gains rate (28%) and the top regular tax rate (39.6%) now reaching close to 12 percentage points, investing for the long-term makes more sense than ever before. Investments in growth stocks and funds that will be taxed at the lower capital gains rate take on added appeal. *And don't overlook the opportunity for outright tax refunds.* Because the Act repeals the 10% excise tax on most luxury goods retroactively to January 1, 1993, you may be entitled to a refund if you purchased such goods earlier in the year.

The Act also retroactively reinstates the health insurance deduction for self-employed individuals. Taxpayers who filed a 1992 tax return claiming the deduction for premiums paid for only the first half of 1992 should consider filing an amended return to claim the deduction for all premiums paid in the last half of 1992.

Business taxpayers are potentially affected by many changes in the areas of deductions, employee benefits, foreign provisions, tax credits, depreciation, alternative minimum tax, etc., etc. This book analyzes all of these new provisions and provides practical commentary to assist you in planning.

Although this book is intended to help you understand how the new tax law will affect your decisions about your personal financial affairs and your business operations, you should also read it with the future in mind. You should begin preparing your financial affairs now with an eye to maximizing long-term growth—which means minimizing the tax bite under the new tax law.

Ernst + Young

August 10, 1993

OVERVIEW OF MAJOR TAX CHANGES

Items of Interest to Individuals

REGULAR TAX RATES

◆ Prior Law

Three statutory tax rates applied to individuals: 15%, 28%, and 31%. For 1993, the top statutory rate of 31% was effective for taxable income exceeding the following amounts based on filing status:

- $53,500 (single)
- $76,400 (head of household)
- $89,150 (married filing jointly)
- $44,575 (married filing separately)

Long-term capital gains were taxed at a maximum rate of 28%.

◆ New Law

A fourth tax bracket of 36% applies to taxable income exceeding the following amounts based on filing status:

- $115,000 (single)
- $127,500 (head of household)
- $140,000 (married filing jointly)
- $70,000 (married filing separately)

A 10% surtax applies to certain high-income taxpayers. It is computed by applying a 39.6% rate to taxable income in excess of the following amounts:

- $250,000 (all individuals, except married filing separately)
- $125,000 (married filing separately)

Long-term capital gains continue to be subject to a maximum rate of 28%.

Effective Date

Tax years beginning after 1992. Additional 1993 taxes which are attributable to the tax increase may be paid in three annual installments.

ITEMIZED DEDUCTIONS AND PERSONAL EXEMPTIONS

◆ Prior Law

For 1993, itemized deductions are reduced by 3% of the excess of adjusted gross income over $108,450 ($54,225 if married filing separately). This limitation is applied *after* any other limitations (e.g., 2% of AGI for miscellaneous itemized deductions). The total of a taxpayer's otherwise allowable deductions cannot be reduced by more than

80% as a result of the 3% limitation. Medical expenses; casualty, theft, and gambling losses; and investment interest expense are not subject to the 3% rule on itemized deductions. This provision was to lapse after 1995.

The tax benefit of the personal and dependent exemptions is phased out for a taxpayer whose adjusted gross income exceeds the amounts specified below, adjusted annually for inflation. For 1993, the phase-out is accomplished by reducing the exemption amount by 2% for each $2,500 of AGI in excess of:

- $108,450 (single)
- $135,600 (head of household)
- $162,700 (married filing jointly)
- $ 81,350 (married filing separately)

This provision was to lapse after 1996.

◆ New Law

The limitation on itemized deductions and the rule phasing out personal exemptions for a taxpayer with AGI above the threshold amount have been made permanent.

TAXATION OF SOCIAL SECURITY BENEFITS

◆ Prior Law

A portion of Social Security benefits is includible in the gross income of a taxpayer whose *provisional income* exceeds a threshold amount. For purposes of this computation, a taxpayer's provisional income includes adjusted gross income plus tax-exempt interest plus certain foreign-source income plus **50%** of the taxpayer's Social Security benefits received. The threshold amount is $25,000 for unmarried taxpayers, $32,000 for taxpayers filing joint returns, and zero for married taxpayers filing separate returns. A taxpayer was required to include in gross income the lesser of (1) 50% of the taxpayer's Social Security benefit, or (2) 50% of the excess of the taxpayer's provisional income over the applicable threshold amount.

◆ New Law

Generally, prior law applies to affected recipients with provisional income below a threshold of $34,000 for unmarried individuals and $44,000 for married individuals. Above those thresholds, up to 85% of Social Security benefits is taxable.

Effective Date

Tax years beginning after 1993.

MEDICARE TAX

◆ Prior Law

Employers and employees each pay a 1.45% Medicare hospital insurance tax (2.9% for self-employed individuals) on a base amount of earned income that is indexed annually for inflation. For 1993, the Medicare tax earned income base is $135,000. Thus, the maximum Medicare tax for an employee is $1,958, and $3,916 for a self-employed individual.

◆ New Law

The dollar limit on wages and self-employment income subject to Medicare taxes for wages and other earned income received **after 1993** has been eliminated. Thus, the 1.45% rate for employees (2.9% for self-employed individuals) will apply to all earned income beginning in 1994.

HEALTH INSURANCE DEDUCTION (25%) FOR SELF-EMPLOYED INDIVIDUALS

◆ Prior Law

Until the provision lapsed on 6/30/92, self-employed individuals could deduct 25% of the amount paid for health insurance premiums for themselves and their spouses and dependents. The deduction also was available to more-than-2% shareholders of S corporations. A deduction is not allowed if the self-employed individual or his/her spouse was eligible for employer-paid health insurance.

◆ New Law

The deduction has been extended through 1993. Taxpayers who filed a 1992 tax return claiming the deduction for premiums paid for only the first half of 1992 **should** consider filing an amended return to claim the deduction for all premiums paid in the last half of 1992.

Effective Date

Tax years ending after 6/30/92.

ALTERNATIVE MINIMUM TAX

◆ Prior Law

The alternative minimum tax system parallels the regular tax system. The AMT rate was a flat 24% with exemptions of $30,000 (single and head of household), $40,000 (married filing jointly), and $20,000 (married filing separately). The exemption phases out when AMT income exceeds defined amounts. To the extent the AMT tax liability exceeds regular tax liability, AMT is imposed.

◆ New Law

There are two AMT rates: a 26% rate applies to the first $175,000 of alternative minimum taxable income, and a 28% rate applies to AMTI in excess of $175,000 ($87,500 for married individuals filing separately). The exemption amounts have been increased to $45,000 (married filing jointly), $33,750 (single and heads of household), and $22,500 (married filing separately and estates and trusts).

Effective Date

Tax years beginning after 1992.

GIFTS OF APPRECIATED PROPERTY

◆ Prior Law

For purposes of the regular income tax the deduction for charitable contributions of appreciated long-term capital gain property (real, personal, or intangible) is allowed to the extent of its fair market value. For purposes of computing the alternative minimum tax (AMT), the deduction for charitable contributions of appreciated long-term capital gain property was allowed only to the extent of the adjusted basis of the property. However, in the case of a contribution of appreciated long-term capital gain *tangible personal property* made before 7/1/92, a deduction was allowed to the extent of the fair market value of the property for AMT purposes.

◆ New Law

The deduction allowable for a contribution of appreciated long-term capital gain property is the same for regular tax and AMT purposes, and generally equals the full fair market value of the contributed property. This eliminates a substantial deterrent to property contributions to art galleries, museums, etc., for those subject to the AMT.

Effective Date

Contributions of tangible personal property made after 7/1/92 and contributions of all other property made after 1992.

ESTATE AND GIFT TAX RATES

◆ Prior Law

For 1993, the top statutory estate tax rate was 50% on estates (and accumulated taxable gifts) in excess of $2.5 million. A phase-out rate of 55% applies between $10.0 million and $18.34 million.

◆ New Law

The top statutory estate tax rates are 53% on estates over $2.5 million but not over $3 million and 55% on estates of $3 million or higher.

The phase-out of the graduated rates and unified credit occurs between $10 million and $21 million. The tax rate on generation-skipping transfers is 55%.

Effective Date

Decedents dying and transfers made after 1992.

REPEAL OF LUXURY EXCISE TAX

◆ Prior Law

A 10% excise tax was imposed on the portion of the retail price of the following items exceeding specified thresholds: automobiles, above $30,000; boats, above $100,000; aircraft, above $250,000; jewelry, above $10,000; and furs, above $10,000.

◆ New Law

The luxury tax for airplanes, boats, furs, and jewelry has been repealed. From August 10, 1993, forward the threshold for luxury automobiles is indexed for inflation occurring after 1990.

Effective Date

Generally, sales after 1992. **This may give rise to refund opportunities for certain individuals who purchased taxable items prior to enactment in 1993.**

Items of Interest to Business

CORPORATE TAX RATES

◆ Prior Law

The top corporate tax rate was 34% and the benefits of lower rate brackets were phased out beginning at $100,000.

◆ New Law

The top corporate rate is increased from 34% to 35% on taxable income (including capital gains) in excess of $10 million. The benefit of lower rate brackets is phased out beginning at $15 million of taxable income.

Effective Date

Tax years beginning after 1992. A fiscal year corporation is required to use a blended rate for its fiscal year that includes January 1, 1993.

CORPORATE ESTIMATED TAXES

◆ Prior Law

Large corporations were required to base estimated tax payments on 97% of current-year tax liability.

◆ New Law

Estimated tax payments are required to be based on 100% of current-year tax liability. In addition, the annualization rules are modified by adding a third set of periods over which corporations may elect to annualize income and by requiring corporations to annually elect which of the three periods they will use to annualize income for the year.

Effective Date

Tax years beginning after 1993.

MOVING EXPENSE DEDUCTION

◆ Prior Law

Generally, if a taxpayer's new job was at least 35 miles farther from the former residence than his or her former job, the taxpayer was permitted an itemized deduction for certain moving expenses incurred in connection with starting work at the new location. These expenses included the cost of meals consumed while traveling and while living in temporary quarters near the new workplace, and the cost of selling (or settling an unexpired lease on) the old residence and buying (or acquiring a lease on) the new residence.

◆ New Law

The mileage threshold is increased from 35 miles to 50 miles. Reimbursed moving expenses are excluded from income; unreimbursed moving expenses are above-the-line deductions. Deductible moving expenses only include the expense of transporting the taxpayer (and members of the taxpayer's household) to the new residence, as well as the cost of moving household goods and personal affects. Deductible moving expenses no longer include the following: the costs of meals; the costs of pre-move househunting trips; the costs of temporary living expenses; the costs incident to the sale or lease of the old residence; and the costs incident to the purchase or lease of a new residence.

Effective Date

Expenses incurred after 1993.

BUSINESS MEALS AND ENTERTAINMENT

◆ Prior Law

Subject to certain exceptions (e.g., expenses treated as compensation and included in gross income), the deduction for meals and entertainment expenses was limited to 80% of the amount incurred.

◆ New Law

The deductible portion of business meals and entertainment expenses is 50%.

Effective Date

Tax years beginning after 1993.

CLUB DUES

◆ Prior Law

If a taxpayer established that his or her use of a club (e.g., a country club) was primarily to further a trade or business, the taxpayer could claim a deduction for the allocable portion of club dues related to the active conduct of the trade or business. Initiation fees and other capital expenditures paid to a club could not be deducted.

◆ New Law

Generally, no deduction is allowed for club dues. This rule applies to luncheon clubs as well as all social clubs. Specific business expenses (e.g., meals) incurred at a club are deductible only to the extent that they otherwise satisfy current law standards for deductibility.

Effective Date

Expenses paid or incurred after 1993.

SMALL BUSINESS EQUIPMENT EXPENSING ELECTION

◆ Prior Law

In lieu of depreciation, a taxpayer with a sufficiently small amount of annual investment in tangible personal property could elect to deduct up to $10,000 of the cost of qualifying property placed in service for the tax year. The $10,000 amount is reduced (but not below zero) by the amount by which the cost of qualifying property placed in service during the tax year exceeds $200,000. In addition, the amount eligible to be expensed for a tax year may not exceed the taxpayer's annual taxable income from compensation for services or the active conduct of any trade or business (determined without regard to this provision). Any amount that is not allowed as a deduction because of the taxable income limitation may be carried forward to succeeding tax years (subject to similar limitations).

◆ New Law

The expensing election has been increased from $10,000 to $17,500.

Effective Date

Tax years beginning after 1992.

AMORTIZATION OF GOODWILL AND INTANGIBLE ASSETS

◆ Prior Law

In determining taxable income, a taxpayer is allowed to claim a deduction for depreciation or amortization of the cost or other basis of intangible property used in a trade or business or held for the production of income, provided the property has a limited useful life that can be determined with reasonable accuracy. No depreciation or amortization deductions were allowed for goodwill or going-concern value.

◆ New Law

Generally, *purchased* intangible assets—including goodwill and going concern value, customer lists and workforce in place, and (if acquired as part of a business) customized existing software, covenants not to compete, and patents and copyrights—are amortized over 15 years. Software not acquired in the acquisition of a trade or business is amortizable over 36 months. The following acquired assets are treated as under current law and are not subject to 15-year amortization: interests in corporations, partnerships, trusts or estates; interests in certain financial contracts; interests in land; interests in films, sound recordings, videotapes and books; rights to receive tangible property under contracts; and interests in patents or copyrights.

Purchased mortgage servicing rights that are not acquired as part of the acquisition of a trade or business are amortized on a straight-line basis over nine years.

Effective Date

The provision generally applies to property acquired after 8/10/93, the date of enactment. A taxpayer may elect to apply the provision to property acquired after 7/25/91. Alternatively, a taxpayer may elect to apply present law (rather than the provisions in the bill) to property acquired under a binding written contract in effect on 8/10/93 and at all times thereafter until the property is acquired. The election to apply the provision to intangibles acquired after 7/25/91 must be made on a timely filed return for the first taxable year that ends after 8/10/93.

QUALIFIED RETIREMENT PLAN BENEFITS AND CONTRIBUTIONS

◆ Prior Law

For 1993, the annual compensation limit that can be taken into account for purposes of benefits and contributions under qualified retirement plans is $235,840.

◆ New Law

The compensation cap has been reduced to $150,000. Benefits accrued in prior years in excess of the reduced limit would be grandfathered. The new cap would be indexed annually for inflation in increments of $10,000.

Effective Date

Benefits accruing in plan years beginning after 1993.

EXECUTIVE COMPENSATION DEDUCTION LIMIT

◆ Prior Law

A taxpayer could claim a business deduction for a reasonable allowance for salaries or other compensation for personal services actually rendered. *Reasonable* was determined on a facts-and-circumstances basis.

◆ New Law

Subject to certain exceptions, a publicly held corporation may not take a deduction for compensation in excess of $1 million paid to its chief executive officer or to any of its four most highly compensated officers.

Compensation not taken into account for the $1 million cap includes (1) payments to a tax-qualified plan, (2) fringe benefits that are excludable from the executive's gross income, and (3) qualified performance-based compensation, which includes any compensation that is payable on a commission basis and any performance-based compensation that meets certain independent director and shareholder approval requirements.

Stock options or other stock appreciation rights are treated as qualified performance-based compensation, provided that requirements for independent director and shareholder approval are met.

Effective Date

Generally, compensation that is otherwise deductible to the corporation in a tax year beginning after 1993. Compensation (e.g., stock options) paid under a binding written plan in effect on 2/17/93 is exempt, provided the terms of the plan are not materially modified after that date.

PASSIVE ACTIVITY LOSS LIBERALIZATION

◆ Prior Law

Passive loss rules limit deductions and credits from passive trade or business activities. Deductions attributable to passive activities, to the extent they exceed income from passive activities, generally may not be deducted against other income, such as wages, portfolio income, or business income that is not derived from a passive activity. *Suspended* deductions are carried forward and are treated as deductions from passive activities in each succeeding year. Suspended losses are allowed in full when the taxpayer disposes of the entire interest in the passive activity to an unrelated person.

A special rule permits deduction of up to $25,000 of losses from certain rental real estate activities (even though they are considered passive) if the taxpayer actively participates in them. This special rule is available in full only to a taxpayer with AGI of $100,000 or less and phases out for a taxpayer with AGI between $100,00 and $150,000.

◆ New Law

Active real estate professionals (defined as working more than half of their time in real estate with a minimum of 750 hours and at least a 5% ownership in their employer if they are an employee) are able to offset passive losses against all of their income.

Effective Date

Tax years beginning after 1993.

♦ ♦ ♦ ♦ ♦ ♦ ♦ ♦

THE ECONOMIC IMPACT
OF THE ACT
Questions & Answers

The overall economic impact of the Act will be less positive than its promoters' optimistic promises and less negative than its critics' dire prophecies. Broadly speaking, the economy will be better off in terms of the budget deficit, interest rates, long-term saving and investment, productivity, energy conservation, and long-term economic growth under this Act than it would be if no Act had been passed. However, there is little likelihood that this, or any deficit reduction Act, will generate the promised "jobs, jobs, jobs"—at least in the short run.

There are many unanswered questions regarding effects of the Act. But general answers to some of the most frequently asked questions are given below:

DEFICITS

Q: *Will the Act reduce the budget deficit substantially?*

A: Yes. A cumulative net deficit reduction of roughly $500 billion over the next five years amounts to about one and one-half percent of the total national spending (GDP) projected over this period. (See the chart on page xxxiii.) Most economists would recognize the deficit reduction as a drag on economic growth, but not to the point of sapping all or most of the vigor from the current recovery.

Q: *Will the Act finally alter the pattern of continuing increases in the deficit and debt?*

A: Yes and no. The budget deficit is projected to decline over the next five years in both absolute magnitude (to about $200 billion) and relative to total national output (to about 2.7% of GDP). Thereafter, the budget deficit will increase in both absolute and percentage terms, unless further action is forthcoming.

Although the budget deficit will decline in the short run, the total federal debt will still be increasing. However, the roughly $500 billion in planned deficit reduction will reduce total government borrowing by roughly a third of what it would have been without the Act. This means that the federal debt will increase by *only* $1 trillion in the next five years rather than the $1.5 trillion projected if there were to be no action. A deficit of about $200 billion in FY 1997 would imply that the national debt would grow no faster (relatively) than national output. (The ratio of national debt to GDP provides a rough indication of our ability to service the national debt.) If the 1993 Act is not followed by additional deficit reduction for 1998 and later years, however, we will again see the federal debt rising faster than the nation's capacity to service it.

Q: *Is the $500 billion a "magic" figure?*

A: Yes and no. The late Senator Everett Dirksen, discussing fiscal policy years ago, said, "A billion

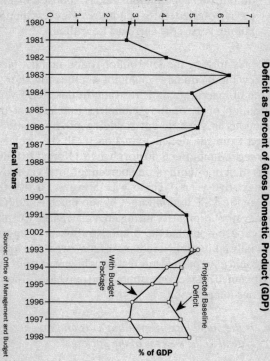

Deficit as Percent of Gross Domestic Product (GDP)

% of GDP

Fiscal Years

With Budget Package

Projected Baseline Deficit

Source: Office of Management and Budget

% of GDP

here, a billion there, and pretty soon it adds up to real money." With economic growth, inflation, and the rise in the public sector, modifying Senator Dirksen's observation by an order of magnitude seems appropriate. (In the mid-1950's, national output was $400 billion, versus almost $6 trillion today; total federal expenditures were less then $50 billion, versus the current $1.5 trillion.)

That is, missing the $500 billion round-number target by a few billion dollars would not significantly alter the degree of macroeconomic restraint in this Act. Even if $20 billion of accounting gimmicks that are not true reductions in government spending programs are removed from the deficit reduction total, the projected macroeconomic effects do not change. (Note: $20 billion is less than one-tenth of one percent of total GDP over the next five years.) There was, however, a risk that missing the $500 billion target by too much could have had a symbolic impact, causing financial markets to alter their expectations that the Administration and Congress are finally taking deficit reduction (somewhat) seriously. This could have pushed interest rates higher and discouraged planned business investment and purchases of homes and consumer durables.

Q: *Is the 50/50 mix of spending cuts and tax increases critical to the success of the package?*

A: Again, yes and no. A dollar of spending reduction and a dollar of taxes will have the same initial impact on the deficit. However, some feared that the package might contain too many tax increases that are generally believed to have a negative impact on the economy. For instance, increases in payroll taxes, capital gains taxes, and corporate income taxes can be expected to adversely affect work and saving habits and business investments. The tax portion of the Act generally avoided, where possible, increasing those taxes thought to have the greatest impacts on savings, investment and economic growth. Similarly, the Act avoided spending cuts in health services, education or other infrastructure investments that could have hurt productivity and long-term growth.

In the short-term, the 50/50 goal is as symbolic as the $500 billion total deficit reduction goal. Altering the 50/50 ratio significantly may have sent the wrong signal to the financial markets, and may have caused interest rates to rise.

Q: *Will we actually achieve these deficit cutting goals?*

A: If we do, it would be an exception to recent budget history. The budget is a forecast based on numerous assumptions. Three of these are critical assumptions which often prove overly optimistic.

- The first is the forecast of future economic growth. The budget act as it stands now assumes that the economy will grow at a real rate of 2.4 to 3.0% annually over the next five years. While this estimate is not as wildly optimistic as projections made in previous budget projections, the likelihood of such steady growth is low.

- The second assumption is that spending programs will be administered as planned. Spending projections don't include certain *add-ons* that occur as judicial and administrative decisions change the way federal programs are administered. Such decisions almost always tend to increase program eligibility or otherwise increase spending over planned levels. However, no contingencies are built into the individual program budgets to accommodate such add-ons. Nor are any contingencies made for unforeseen new programs (for example, major natural disaster relief, responses to financial crises, or emergency defense expenditures.) As Federal Reserve Chairman Alan Greenspan recently testified, "We are understating the longer-term pattern of spending and therefore must find ways to come to grips with the spending question."

- The last assumption is that tax changes will not significantly affect the behavior of individuals and businesses. Although budget planners attempt to take into account the presumed behavioral reactions of individuals and businesses to tax changes, they usually overestimate the revenue generated by a tax increase and overestimate the loss in revenue from a tax cut.

INTEREST RATES AND SHORT-TERM ECONOMIC GROWTH

Q: *Will passage of the Act reduce interest rates?*

A: Probably not much further. Interest rates have already dropped to their lowest levels in recent history, in part because investors became convinced that the Administration and Congress would begin to deal seriously with the deficit. At present, the financial markets expect a $500 billion reduction in the deficit over the next five years. Long-term interest rates already reflect these expectations. Furthermore, Chairman Alan Greenspan has told Congress that the Federal Reserve was also expecting a $500 billion package (as a first tranche of deficit reduction). Therefore, short-term rates are also unlikely to fall as a result of this Act.

Passage does, however, keep both short and long-term interest rates from rising. Had the package failed and no alternative action of equivalent magnitude been forthcoming, the Federal Reserve would be more inclined to nudge up short-term rates. Long-term rates likely would react even more strongly to the specter of the federal government possibly not cutting its borrowing by one third over the next five years.

Q: *Will the reduced short- and long-term interest rates stimulate economic growth in the short run?*

A: All other things being equal, yes. Lower interest rates stimulate business investment and encourage household purchases of homes, autos, appliances and other consumer durables. However, all other things are not equal. Cutting spending and raising taxes also leads to lower economic activity. Therefore, although deficit reduction will lower the cost of borrowing for businesses and households, it may also reduce business and consumer demand. Most economists believe that the contractionary effects of lower deficits are greater than the stimulative effects of the associated lower interest rates, so that the net effect is slower economic growth in the short term. Even so, most public and private forecasters expect moderate economic growth of 2 to 3% over the next year or so.

LONG-TERM SAVING AND INVESTMENT PROSPECTS

Q: *Will the Act induce Americans to save more?*

A: National saving is private (business and household) saving plus government saving. Reduced government borrowing is, in essence, identical to increased government savings. Government saving will thus increase by the full magnitude of the deficit reduction. Private saving, however, can be expected to fall somewhat due to the lower interest rates and higher income taxes. Private saving also will fall as income falls. Nevertheless, expect total saving to increase.

Q: *Will increased national saving improve investment prospects?*

A: Yes. Freeing up $500 billion for private sector borrowing, and hence for investment in the private sector, has the potential to boost net business capital investment in the U.S. back to the levels of the 1960s and 1970s (to about 3.6% of national income). Features of the Act like empowerment zones, increasing the §179 limit for expensing capital expenditures, the small business capital gains tax incentive, and the low-income housing credits will favor some types of investment over others.

PRODUCTIVITY AND INTERNATIONAL COMPETITIVENESS

Q: *Will the "economic stimulus" aspects of the Act help turn around the productivity growth slow-down?*

A: Productivity growth prospects should be enhanced, but not so much from the specific "stimulus" pieces as from the total funds freed up for private investment. A recent study by productivity expert John Kendrick found that about 45% of U.S. productivity growth in the past three decades was accounted for by increases in the overall capital stock. Other contributing factors were education, health and safety, mobility of labor, shifts in the age and gender mix of the workforce, and—most important—technological improvement. Thus, greater private investment can be expected to translate into greater productivity growth. To the extent certain provisions in the Act favor education (e.g., student loan reform) and/or technological investment (e.g., extending the R&D tax credit), the impact on productivity will be more positive.

Q: *How will the Act affect international competitiveness?*

A: A positive effect is likely. Lower U.S. interest rates tend to reduce the value of the dollar relative to foreign currencies. Thus, all other things being equal, U.S. produced goods will become cheaper relative to foreign products. In addition, higher investment and productivity growth should improve the international competitiveness of U.S. businesses over the longer term.

ENERGY CONSERVATION

Q: *Will the energy tax component of the Act help the environmental fight to conserve energy and reduce oil imports?*

A: Not by much. A 4.3-cents-per-gallon rise in the gasoline tax (about 75 cents a week for the average driver) is unlikely to change the driving habits of many Americans in the short-term. Even over a longer horizon, the effects will be minimal. The BTU tax proposed by the Administration was projected to reduce oil import dependence by just 3.5% by 2000, and the gas tax is only one third as large.

LONG-TERM ECONOMIC GROWTH AND JOBS

Q: *Will the Budget Reconciliation Act produce "jobs, jobs, jobs?"*

A: In the short run, no. Economic growth will be restrained and hence job creation will be limited. This Act does, however, improve long-term economic prospects and should therefore, enhance job growth over the longer term.

Q: *Is Clinton's estimate of 8 million new jobs in the next 5 years realistic?*

A: Yes, if the economy grows at 2.5 to 3% annually. In the past decade, the growth in the number of jobs averaged just under 1.2% annually, while real national income grew at an average of greater than

2.5%. If the overall economy grows at 2.5 to 3% over the next five years, then the number of new jobs should be in the 7 to 8 million range. Thus, the target of 8 million new jobs is realistic.

FUTURE TAX AND BUDGET ACTIONS

Q: *What next?*

A: This Act does not provide a permanent solution to the nation's deficit problem. Further actions will be needed to stem the tide of rising deficits after 1997. Health care reform also promises new spending needs if all Americans are to receive medical coverage, as is currently proposed. Other needs are sure to arise. Thus, further spending cuts and tax increases will be necessary in the not-too-distant future.

◆ ◆ ◆ ◆ ◆ ◆ ◆

TABLE OF EFFECTIVE DATES

This table contains the effective dates of the key tax provisions of the Omnibus Budget Reconciliation Act of 1993, arranged alphabetically by subject matter. If a provision has more than one effective date, or if there are exceptions or transitional rules, the table lists the general effective date. For more detailed effective dates, exceptions, and transition rules, refer to the specified page. Note that the Act contains several provisions that are effective retroactively.

Item (page)	Effective Date
Accumulated Earnings and Personal Holding Company Taxes (55)	Tax years beginning after 1992.
Alternative Minimum Tax (Individuals) (28)	Tax years beginning after 1992.
Alternative Minimum Tax Relief (Corporations) (61)	Property placed in service after 1993.
Amortization of Goodwill and Intangible Assets (89)	Property acquired after August 10, 1993. Election for property acquired after July 25, 1991.
Boats—Repeal of Diesel Fuel Exemption (192)	January 1, 1994.
Business Meals and Entertainment (65)	Tax years beginning after 1993.
Cancellation of Indebtedness— Expansion of Tax Attributes Reduced (100)	Tax years beginning after 1993.
Cancellation of Indebtedness— Stock-for-Debt Exception (102)	Stock transferred after 1994.

Item (page)	Effective Date
Capital Gains Generators and Other Conversion Techniques—Limitation (131)	Transactions entered into and obligations acquired after April 30, 1993. Elimination of capital gains from investment income effective for tax years beginning after 1992.
Capital Gains Incentive—Investment in Small Business (43)	Stock issued after August 10, 1993.
Charitable Contributions—Substantiation Requirements (35)	Contributions made on or after January 1, 1994.
Club Dues (68)	Amounts paid or incurred after 1993.
Contributions of Appreciated Property (32)	Contributions of tangible personal property made after June 30, 1992 and contributions of other property made after 1992.
Corporate Estimated Taxes (57)	Tax years beginning after 1993.
Corporate Tax Rates (51)	Tax years beginning on or after January 1, 1993. A fiscal-year corporation is required to use a blended rate for its fiscal year that includes January 1, 1993.
Deferral of Tax on Foreign Earnings (170)	Tax years beginning after September 30, 1993.
Depreciation of Nonresidential Real Property (162)	Property placed in service on or after May 13, 1993.
Diesel Fuel Excise Tax (191)	January 1, 1994.
Discharge of Real Property Indebtedness (153)	Discharges after 1992.
Earned Income Credit (EIC) (19)	Tax years beginning after 1993.
Earnings Stripping and Other Anti-Avoidance Rules (182)	Earnings stripping—Tax years beginning after 1993. Portfolio debt—obligations issued after April 7, 1993.
Employer Credit for FICA Taxes on Tip Income (66)	FICA taxes paid after 1993.

Item (page)	Effective Date
Employer-Provided Educational Assistance (110)	Reinstated retroactively to June 30, 1992 and extended through December 31, 1994.
Empowerment Zones and Enterprise Communities (80)	After December 31, 1993; zones to be designated in 1994 and 1995.
Estimated Taxes— Individuals (25)	Tax years beginning after 1993.
Estate and Gift Tax Rates (38)	Decedents dying and gifts made after 1992.
Executive Compensation— $1,000,000 Deduction Limitation (117)	Amounts otherwise deductible in a tax year beginning on or after January 1, 1994.
Export of Unprocessed Softwood Timber (202)	Dispositions after August 10, 1993.
Federal Assistance Payments Made to Certain Thrifts (129)	Financial assistance credited on or after March 4, 1991, unless received with respect to specified transactions before that date.
Foreign Tax Credit for Oil Multinationals (186)	Tax years beginning after 1992.
Gasoline Tax (192)	October 1, 1993.
Health Insurance Deduction for Self-Employed Individuals (42)	Reinstated retroactively to tax years ending after June 30, 1992. Scheduled to terminate for tax years ending after December 31, 1993.
Individual Regular Tax Rates (1)	Tax years beginning after 1992.
Information Reporting— Discharge of Indebtedness (197)	Discharges after December 31, 1993. Discharges after August 10, 1993 for specified governmental entities.
Intercompany Sales (184)	Tax years beginning after 1993.,
Itemized Deductions (14)	Provision previously set to expire on December 31, 1995; this Act makes provision permanent.
Lobbying Expense Deduction (70)	Amounts paid or incurred after 1993.

Item (page)	Effective Date
Low-Income Rental housing Tax Credit (141)	Extended retroactively to July 1, 1992 and made permanent. Modifications to credit have several effective dates.
Luxury Tax—Repeal (Except Autos) (40)	Sales on or after January 1, 1993. Passenger vehicles purchased after August 10, 1993.
Medicare Tax Increase (23)	Wages and income received after 1993.
Mortgage Revenue Bonds (142)	Reinstated retroactively to July 1, 1992 and made permanent.
Moving Expense Deduction (63)	Expenses incurred after 1993.
Partnership Redemptions (158)	Partners retiring or dying on or after January 5, 1993.
Passive Foreign Investment Companies (170)	Tax years beginning after September 30, 1993.
Passive Loss Liberalization (143)	Tax years beginning after 1993.
Penalty—Accuracy Related (199)	Tax returns due (without regard to extensions) after 1993.
Pension Fund and Other Investments in Real Estate (149)	Exclusion from UBIT effective for property acquired on or after January 1, 1994. Related provisions have several effective dates.
Personal Exemptions (12)	Provision previously set to expire on December 31, 1996; this Act makes provision permanent.
Possession Tax Credit (178)	Tax years beginning after 1993.
Qualified Retirement Plan Benefits and Contributions (113)	Benefits accruing in plan years beginning after 1993.
R&E Expenses— Allocation (168)	The first tax year (beginning on or before August 1, 1994) following the last tax year to which Rev. Proc. 92-56

Item (page)	Effective Date
Refunds—Expansion of 45-Day Interest-Free Period (195)	45-day rule: Returns due (without regard to extensions) on or after January 1, 1994. Amended return rules: Amended returns and claims for refund filed on or after January 1, 1995. IRS-initiated adjustments: Refunds paid on or after January 1, 1995.
Research and Development Credit (76)	Reinstated retroactively to June 30, 1992 and extended through June 30, 1995.
Rollover of Gain from Sale of Publicly Traded Securities into Specialized Small Business Investment Companies (48)	Sales on or after August 10, 1993.
Section 956 (Investment of Earnings in U.S. Property)—Modifications (174)	Tax years beginning after September 30, 1993
Securities Dealers—Mark to Market Inventory (121)	Tax years ending on or after December 31, 1993.
Small Business Equipment Expensing Election (78)	Tax years beginning after 1992.
Small Issue Manufacturing and Farmers Bonds (202)	Reinstated retroactively for bonds issued after June 30, 1992 and made permanent.
Social Security Benefits—Taxation (16)	Tax years beginning after 1993.
Subpart F—Other Modifications (171)	Tax years beginning after September 30, 1993.
Surtax on High-Income Taxpayers (1)	Tax years beginning after 1992.
Targeted Jobs Tax Credit (112)	Reinstated retroactively to June 30, 1992 and extended through December 31, 1994.
Transfer Pricing Compliance (164)	Tax years beginning after 1993.
Transportation Fuels Tax (189)	October 1, 1993.
Travel Expenses for Spouses and Dependents (74)	Amounts paid or incurred after 1993.
Withholding on Supplemental Wages (79)	Payments made after 1993.

1

◆ ◆ ◆ ◆ ◆ ◆ ◆

CHANGES OF CONCERN TO INDIVIDUALS

REGULAR TAX RATE INCREASES AND CAPITAL GAINS RATE

◆ Prior Law

Three tax rates applied to ordinary taxable income of individuals: 15%, 28%, and 31%. The taxable income brackets for 1993 are shown on page 2.

The top tax rate on net capital gains — the excess of net long-term capital gains over net short-term capital losses — was capped at 28%. The individual income tax brackets were indexed each year for inflation.

◆ New Law

The Act establishes two additional tax brackets: a 36% bracket, and a 10% *surtax* on higher-income taxpayers which results in a 39.6% top bracket. These rates apply only to ordinary income, including wages, earnings from self-employment, inter-

Taxable Income Brackets for 1993 (old law)

Tax Rates	Single	Married/Joint	Married/Separate	Head of Household
15%	$0–22,100	$0–36,900	$0–18,450	$0–29,600
28%	$22,100–53,500	$36,900–89,150	$18,450–44,575	$29,600–76,400
31%	Over $53,500	Over $89,150	Over $44,575	Over $76,400

Rate Levels Taking Effect Beginning January 1, 1993 (new law)

Tax Rates	Single	Married/Joint	Married/Separate	Head of Household
15%	$0–22,100	$0–36,900	$0–18,450	$0–29,600
28%	$22,100–53,500	$36,900–89,150	$18,450–44,575	$29,600–76,400
31%	$53,500–115,000	$89,150–140,000	$44,575–70,000	$76,400–127,500
36%	$115,000–250,000	$140,000–250,000	$70,000–125,000	$127,500–250,000
39.6%	Over $250,000	Over $250,000	Over $125,000	Over $250,000

est, dividends, and net short-term capital gains. The top tax rate on net capital gains remains at 28%.

The new rate levels will take effect retroactively ***beginning January 1, 1993*** as shown on page 2.

The following chart illustrates 1993 tax rates and taxable income brackets under prior law and the new law for a married couple filing a joint return.

As under prior law, the tax brackets will continue to be indexed annually for inflation. How-

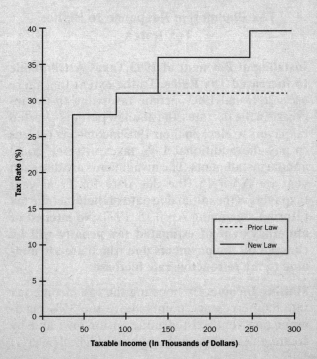

Composition of Tax Rates and Brackets Under Prior Law and New Law for Joint Filers

ever, indexing of the 36% and 39.6% brackets will not begin until 1995. Withholding tables for 1993 will not be revised to reflect the changes in tax rates. Accordingly, penalties for underpayment of estimated taxes will be waived for underpayments of 1993 taxes attributable to these changes in tax rates.

EXAMPLE: The impact of the new higher ordinary income rates on married taxpayers filing joint returns is illustrated in the chart on page 5.

Tax Planning in Response to Higher Tax Rates

Installment Payment of 1993 Taxes Attributable to Increased Tax Rates. To the extent that there are additional 1993 income taxes due to the increase in the tax rates, the new law permits affected taxpayers to elect on their 1993 income tax returns to pay the additional 1993 taxes in three equal annual installments. The installments are due each year on April 15 (the due date for fiscal year taxpayers is the initial due date of their income tax returns), beginning April 15, 1994. **No interest or underpayment of estimated tax penalty will be charged on the payments due which are attributable to the retroactive rate increase.**

Shifting Income. By boosting the top income tax rate 8.6 percentage points above the 31% maximum rate that existed under prior law, and by creating a 24.6% spread between the highest (39.6%)

Impact of the Tax Act on Joint Filers in 1993

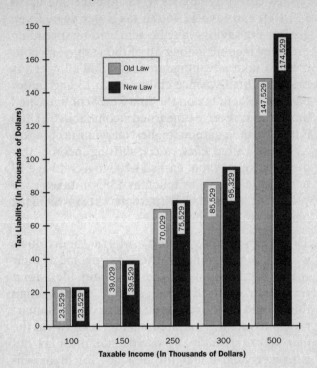

and lowest (15%) marginal tax rates, the new tax law enhances the tax savings that can be realized by shifting income. Higher-income parents should consider transferring assets that generate ordinary income, such as dividends and interest, to children age 14 or older in order to take advantage of their lower tax bracket. For example, shifting $10,000 of investment income from a parent in the 39.6% tax bracket to a child over 13 who is in the 15% bracket (which currently applies to taxable income up to $22,100) can save $2,460 in taxes per year. Even greater tax savings may be achieved by spreading ordinary income among all of the taxpayer's children to take advantage of each child's lower tax bracket. Finally, since children age 13 and under pay only $90 in tax on the first $1,200 of unearned income they receive (unearned income above $1,200 is taxed at their parents' highest marginal tax bracket ... the so-called *kiddie tax*), shifting income-producing property that earns $1,200 to a child age 13 or under can save as much as $385 in taxes each year [($1,200 × 39.6%) (parents' rate) – $90 (tax paid by the child)].

The *Marriage Tax Penalty*. Married individuals who earn approximately the same income as their spouses typically pay more tax if they file a joint return (or married filing separate returns) than they would if they could file returns as two unmarried individuals. This phenomenon is known as the *marriage tax penalty*. It existed under prior law but is exacerbated under the new law for higher-income spouses. The chart on page 7 shows the effect of the marriage tax penalty in the context of the new tax rates.

Couples who are planning a late-in-the-year wedding and have similar incomes may wish to consider postponing the marriage to the next year in order to avoid the marriage tax penalty for one more year. Conversely, divorcing spouses with similar incomes should consider finalizing the divorce be-

Marriage Penalty

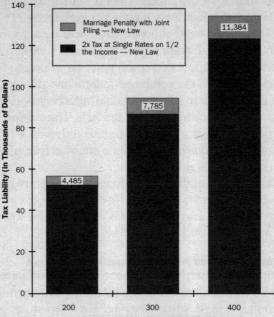

fore the end of the year in order to escape a year's worth of marriage tax penalty.

Tax-Exempt Investments. The higher income tax rates under the new law should increase the appeal of tax-exempt bonds and bond funds, especially for taxpayers in the 39.6% top marginal tax bracket. As tax rates rise, taxable securities must provide a higher yield in order to match the yield offered by tax-exempt bonds of similar quality and time to maturity. For example, to a taxpayer in the 31% bracket, a taxable bond yielding 8.69% is comparable to a municipal bond with a 6.0% tax-exempt yield. However, a taxpayer in the new 39.6% bracket would need almost a 10% yield on a taxable bond to match the municipal bond's 6.0% return. And considering the fact that some states have income tax rates over 10%, the combined federal and state marginal tax rate, taking phase-outs and other *back door* tax increases into account, can exceed 50%. Thus, an investor living in such a high tax state would need a 12% taxable bond to achieve the same after-tax return as a 6% municipal bond.

The following table demonstrates the yield you would have to earn on a taxable bond in order to generate the same after-tax earnings as a tax-exempt bond would provide at a correspondingly lower yield.

Equivalent Yield Needed from a Taxable Bond

Tax-Exempt Yield	*Your Combined Federal, State & Local Marginal Tax Bracket*						
	28%	**31%**	**33%**	**36%**	**39.6%**	**42%**	**46%**
4.00	5.56	5.80	5.97	6.25	6.62	6.90	7.41
4.50	6.25	6.52	6.72	7.03	7.45	7.76	8.33
5.00	6.94	7.25	7.46	7.81	8.28	8.62	9.26
5.50	7.64	7.97	8.21	8.59	9.11	9.48	10.19
6.00	8.33	8.70	8.96	9.38	9.93	10.34	11.11
6.50	9.03	9.42	9.70	10.16	10.76	11.21	12.04
7.00	9.72	10.15	10.45	10.94	11.59	12.07	12.96

Tax Deferral Plans. The new higher tax rates may also enhance the benefits of deferred compensation plans and other tax-deferral arrangements, particularly if the taxpayer anticipates being in a lower tax bracket when the income is eventually received. For example, the tax-deferred buildup offered by 401(k) plans, individual retirement accounts, Keogh plans, other retirement plans, and life insurance policies that offer inside cash buildup may now be more attractive.

Ordinary Versus Capital Gains Rates. With the top rate on ordinary income rising to 39.6% and the maximum tax rate on net capital gains fixed at 28%, the new tax law creates an 11.6 percentage point differential between the top individual rates on ordinary income and capital gains. Under prior law, there was only a 3 point differential between the 31% top rate on ordinary income and the 28% maximum rate on net capital gains. This widened tax rate differential may encourage high-income individuals to favor investments geared toward appreciation that will be taxed at the lower 28% capital gains rate when the investments are sold over investments that generate current interest and dividends, which would be taxed at a 36% or 39.6% rate. Not surprisingly, the new law contains several new provisions which limit or eliminate the ability of taxpayers to realize capital gain income in transactions which generated capital gains under prior law. These provisions affect so-called *conversion transactions*, the tax treatment of market discount on tax-exempt bonds and taxable bonds issued on or before July 18, 1984, and the tax treatment of stripped preferred stock. Henceforth, gains from these transactions will generally be treated as ordinary income.

The widening gap between the top tax rates on ordinary income and capital gains is likely to enhance the attractiveness of incentive stock options (ISOs) to executives compared to nonqualified stock options (NSOs). The key is the differing tax treatment of the *option spread*—the difference between the fair market value of the stock at the time of exercise and the exercise price. ISOs do not trigger taxable income until the stock received from exercising the option is sold. Exercising an ISO does, however, result in income for alternative minimum tax purposes and, therefore, may trigger the alternative minimum tax (see discussion on page 28). Careful planning should be undertaken in this regard. Further, if ISO stock is sold at least one year after the date of exercise *and* two years following the date the ISO was granted, the difference between the sale price and exercise price is taxed as a long-term capital gain at the 28% rate. By contrast, the recipient of an NSO will generally recognize compensation income when the NSO is exercised, which could be taxed as much as 39.6% under the new law.

Trusts and Estates. The new tax rates hit trusts and estates in two ways. Top tax rates have been hiked to 36% and 39.6%, and the tax brackets at which the new higher rates apply have been lowered. For example, under prior law, the 31% rate applied to taxable income over $11,250. Now, the 36% rate is imposed on taxable income between $5,500 and $7,500.

The chart below compares the tax rates and income brackets for trusts and estates under prior and new law:

Trusts/Estates

Tax Rates	Prior law	New Law
15%	0–$3,750	$0–1,500
28%	$3,750–11,250	$1,500–3,500
31%	Over $11,250	$3,500–5,500
36%	Not applicable	$5,500– 7,500
39.6%	Not applicable	Over $7,500

The new law's compression of tax brackets to the point where the 39.6% tax rate applies to trust taxable income over $7,500, in most cases, will make it impractical or even disadvantageous to retain income in a trust as a tax-savings device.

In response to the increased tax rates and compressed brackets, fiduciaries may wish (or effectively be compelled) to consider:

- Making distributions to beneficiaries of complex trusts in order to spread income across lower tax brackets. For example, single filers do not face the new 36% bracket until their taxable income exceeds $115,000. However, distributions will not necessarily escape the higher tax rates if the beneficiary is under age 14 and is therefore subject to the *kiddie tax* on unearned income at his or her parents' highest marginal tax rate. Furthermore, the trust document or the wishes of the grantor may limit the trustee's discretion to make distributions, particularly when minors are beneficiaries.

- Shifting trust assets away from investments that generate ordinary taxable income (e.g., interest and dividends) to tax-exempt instruments or investments that provide capital appreciation. Of course, the desire to minimize federal taxes should not generally be the primary factor in making investment decisions.

PHASE-OUT OF PERSONAL EXEMPTIONS

◆ Prior Law

For 1993, a taxpayer can claim a $2,350 exemption for each dependent. However, each personal and dependent exemption claimed is simultaneously reduced at the rate of 2% per $2,500 increment ($1,250 for a married individual filing a separate return)—or fraction thereof—of adjusted gross income in excess of specified thresholds. The applicable threshold depends on a taxpayer's filing status:

1993 Adjusted Gross Income Thresholds for the Phase-out of Personal Exemptions

Married/ Joint	Head of Household	Single	Married/ Separate
$162,700	$135,600	$108,450	$81,350

These thresholds are indexed annually for inflation. The phase-out of personal exemptions was scheduled to expire after 1996.

◆ New Law

The phase-out of personal exemptions is extended permanently, and the thresholds are indexed annually for inflation.

EXAMPLE: Mr. and Mrs. Green file a joint return in 1993, reporting AGI of $250,000. They claim two personal exemptions. Because their AGI exceeds their applicable threshold of $162,700 by $87,300, each of their personal exemptions is reduced by $1,645 (($87,300/$2,500 rounded up) × 2% × $2,350

= $1,645). Thus, the amount of each exemption is only $705 ($2,350−$1,645), or $1,410 for two exemptions.

Commentary: The impact of this provision for affected taxpayers is the same as if their marginal tax rate were increased. It raises the new 36% rate by about .68%, and the new 39.6% rate by .74%, for *each* exemption claimed. Thus, a taxpayer in the new 39.6% bracket with four exemptions will pay tax at an effective marginal rate of 42.56% after the phase-out is taken into account.

LIMITATION ON ITEMIZED DEDUCTIONS

◆ Prior Law

Taxpayers who do not elect the standard deduction can itemize their deductions in arriving at taxable income. However, certain itemized deductions (interest, taxes, losses, charitable contributions and certain miscellaneous expenses) are reduced regardless of the taxpayer's filing status by 3% of the excess of the taxpayer's adjusted gross income over a specified amount. In 1993, this amount is $108,450 ($54,225 for a married individual filing a separate return). The floor is indexed annually for inflation. This means that a taxpayer with AGI of $170,000 would lose $1,846 [($170,000−$108,450) × 3%)] of itemized deductions.

This overall limitation is imposed *after* any other limitations affecting specific categories of itemized deductions are applied. For example, miscellaneous itemized deductions are first reduced by an amount equal to 2% of the taxpayer's AGI and are then subject to the additional 3% phase-out. However, medical expenses, casualty, theft and gambling losses, and investment interest expense are exempt from the 3% limitation.

EXAMPLE: Suppose the Greens have adjusted gross income of $200,000 in 1993, and that their miscellaneous itemized deductions in 1993 total $25,000. This amount is first reduced by the 2% of adjusted gross income floor for miscellaneous itemized deductions: $25,000−(2% × $200,000) = $21,000. The overall limitation is then applied to further reduce the Green's itemized deductions by $2,746 to $18,254 [21,000−(3% × $200,000−$108,450)].

The total of a taxpayer's otherwise allowable deductions cannot be reduced by more than 80% as a result of the 3% limitation. Additionally, the limitation does not apply in determining the amount of a taxpayer's alternative minimum tax.

This provision was scheduled to lapse after 1995.

◆ **New Law**

The limitation on itemized deductions is extended permanently.

> *Commentary:* For affected taxpayers, this provision effectively increases the new 36% and 39.6% marginal rates by up to 1.08% and 1.19%, respectively.

TAXATION OF SOCIAL SECURITY BENEFITS

◆ **Prior Law**

A portion of an individual's Social Security benefits is subject to income tax to the extent that the taxpayer's *provisional income* exceeds the following thresholds: $32,000 in the case of a married individual filing a joint return, $0 if married filing separately, unless he or she lived apart from his or her spouse for the entire taxable year; and $25,000 in the case of all other individuals. *Provisional income* is comprised of adjusted gross income plus tax-exempt interest, certain foreign source income, and one-half of Social Security benefits received. The amount of benefits taxed is the lesser of one-half the benefits received, or one-half of the amount by which provisional income exceeds the applicable threshold.

◆ New Law

The new law creates a second tier of Social Security benefit inclusion in gross income. Existing rules for calculating the amount of Social Security benefits subject to income tax remain the same for unmarried filers with provisional income between $25,000 and $34,000, and for joint filers with provisional income between $32,000 and $44,000.

For taxpayers with provisional income in excess of the new higher thresholds, the portion of Social Security benefits received that is subject to tax is calculated as *the lesser of:*

- 85% of Social Security benefits received; or

- The sum of the following amounts:

  a. The smaller of (1) the amount that would have been included in income under prior law; or (2) $4,500 (for unmarried taxpayers) or $6,000 (for married taxpayers filing joint returns), plus

  b. 85% of the excess of the taxpayer's provisional income over the new threshold amount.

For married individuals filing separately, taxable Social Security benefits are calculated as the lesser of 85% of benefits received or 85% of the taxpayer's provisional income.

The table below illustrates the portion of $10,000 in Social Security benefits received that would be includible in the taxable income of single and joint filers at various income levels.

Amount of $10,000 in Social Security Benefits Included in Taxable Income

Provisional Income	Single	Joint
$25,000	None	None
34,000	$4,500	$1,000
38,000	7,900	3,000
44,000	8,500	5,000
50,000	8,500	8,500

Effective Date

Tax years beginning after December 31, 1993.

Commentary: Under prior law, up to one-half of a taxpayer's Social Security benefits were subject to tax. The new law taxes up to 85% of benefits received, which represents a significant tax increase for middle income retirees. The added tax burden means that certain Social Security recipients would benefit from shifting some of their investments from income-producing assets to investments that favor capital appreciation. They may defer recognition of income by investing, for example, in U.S. Savings Bonds. If they never cash in the bonds, their heirs will recognize the income. Alternatively, they may stagger the recognition of U.S. bond (or other) income so that they create alternating years of high and low income. Under the right circumstances, an individual may reduce the amount of Social Security benefits taxed in the *low-income* years without increasing the amount of benefits that otherwise would have been taxed in the *high-income* years For those retirees with income between $25,000 and $50,000 such planning may be useful.

EARNED INCOME TAX CREDIT

◆ Prior Law

The earned income tax credit (EITC) is a refundable credit available to lower-income workers. To qualify for the credit, taxpayers are required to have at least one *qualifying* child living with them. The EITC is comprised of three different credits: (1) the basic credit; (2) a supplemental credit for children under the age of one; and (3) a supplemental credit for health insurance premiums paid for qualifying children.

In 1993, the EITC basic credit is 18.5% of the first $7,750 of earned income (19.5% for a taxpayer with two or more qualifying children). The maximum basic credit is therefore $1,434 ($1,511 for taxpayers with two or more qualifying children). The maximum credit is reduced by 13.21% (13.93% for workers with two or more qualifying children) of the excess of earned income (or adjusted gross income — AGI — if greater) over $12,200. For example, a taxpayer with one child and earned income of $15,000 would be entitled to an earned income tax credit of $1,064 [maximum of $1,434 less (13.21% × ($15,000 – $12,200))].

The maximum supplemental young child (under one year old) credit is $388 in 1993. This amount is based on 5% of the first $7,750 of earned income. It phases out at a 3.57% rate applied to earned income (or AGI, if greater) over $12,200.

The maximum supplemental health insurance credit in 1993 is $465. This amount is based on 6% of the first $7,750 of earned income. It phases out at a 4.285% rate applied to earned income (or AGI, if greater) over $12,200.

◆ New Law

The supplemental young child and health insurance credits have been repealed and a larger basic credit is available. The basic credit is also now available to low-income workers who do not have children, are between ages 25 and 65, and are not claimed as a dependent by another taxpayer.

The basic earned income tax rates, earned income levels upon which the credit is figured, and rates and income ranges at which the credit phases out are summarized in the table on page 22.

Effective Date

Tax years beginning after December 31, 1993.

Commentary: For affected taxpayers, the increased credit effectively reduces their overall tax under the new law. Note that the credit rate (7.65%) for individuals without qualifying children is the same as the employee share of FICA (Social Security) taxes on their wages. Thus, the EITC effectively refunds those taxes for wages up to $4,000 per year. Eligible taxpayers can receive their EITC credit (1) all at once in the form of a refund by attaching Schedule EIC to their income tax return for the year or (2) in *advance payments* included in their regular paychecks *during* the current tax year. Available advance payments are limited. The limitation is figured on 60% of the maximum credit available to taxpayers with one qualifying child. Therefore, available advance payments are limited to about $1,220 in 1994. To receive advance payments, a taxpayer must fill out Form W-5, *Earned Income Credit Advance Payment Certificate,* and give it to his or her employer. Congress is requiring the Internal Revenue Service to institute a test program over the next two years to notify taxpayers with qualifying

Year	Number of Qualifying Children	Credit Rate	Earned Income Levels[1]	Maximum Credit	Phase-out Rate	Phase-out Applies to Earned Income/ AGI Over[1]	Credit Not Available When Earned Income/ AGI Exceeds[1]
1994	None	7.65%	$0–4,000	$306	7.65%	$5,000	$9,000
	One	26.30%	0–7,750	2,038	15.98%	11,000	23,750
	Two or more	30.00%	0–8,425	2,527	17.68%	11,000	25,290
1995	None	7.65%	$0–4,110[2]	314[2]	7.65%	5,140[2]	9,240[2]
	One	34.0%	0–6,170[2]	2,098[2]	15.98%	11,300[2]	24,430[2]
	Two or more	36.0%	0–8,650[2]	3,115[2]	20.22%	11,300[2]	26,710[2]
1996 and after	None	7.65%	$0–4,200[2]	323[2]	7.65%	5,270[2]	9,490[2]
	One	34.0%	0–6,330[2]	2,152[2]	15.98%	11,600[2]	25,070[2]
	Two or more	40.0%	0–8,890[2]	3,556[2]	21.06%	11,600[2]	28,490[2]

[1] To be adjusted annually for inflation (estimated to be 2.7%) after 1994.
[2] Estimated for projected inflation.

22

children about the availability of advance EITC payments.

MEDICARE TAX INCREASE

◆ Prior Law

Employers and employees each pay a 1.45% Medicare hospital insurance tax (2.9% for self-employed individuals) on a base amount of earned income that is indexed annually for inflation. For 1993, the Medicare tax earned income base is $135,000. Thus, the maximum Medicare tax for an employee is $1,958 and $3,916 for a self-employed individual.

◆ New Law

The dollar limit on wages and self-employment income subject to Medicare taxes for wages and other earned income received after 1993 has been eliminated. Thus, the 1.45% rate for employees (2.9% for self-employed individuals) will apply to all earned income beginning in 1994.

Effective Date

Wages and salary or self-employment earnings received after December 31, 1993.

EXAMPLE: The table below demonstrates the impact of eliminating the Medicare wage base cap on highly compensated employees. Under prior law, Medicare taxes were capped at $1,958 ($135,000 × 1.45%).

Gross Wages	Prior Law	New Law	% Increase
$125,000	$1,813	$1,813	0%
150,000	1,958	2,175	11%
250,000	1,958	3,625	85%
350,000	1,958	5,075	159%
1,000,000	1,958	14,500	641%

Commentary: This provision effectively adds an extra 1.45% (2.9% with respect to self-employment earnings) to the new 36% and 39.6% marginal tax rates. In effect, the marginal rates on wages rise to 37.45% and 41.05% (38.9% and 42.5% on self-employment earnings), respectively. **If you take into account this Medicare tax increase along with the phase-outs of personal exemptions and itemized deductions, a married taxpayer with two children earning over $250,000 may have a top 1994 marginal rate of 45.2%.**

Since the repeal of the Medicare earnings cap does not take effect until 1994, individuals who otherwise expect self-employment income in 1993 in excess of the $135,000 Medicare cap may find it advantageous to accelerate such earnings (e.g., through advance billings, etc.) into this year. The accelerated income will escape the Medicare tax that otherwise would have been charged if the earnings were realized next year. On the other hand, *income tax* must be paid sooner on any accelerated earnings.

Accelerating self-employment income to save Medicare taxes should not be pursued in a vacuum—any actions taken should make overall financial sense. Therefore, taxpayers should weigh the Medicare tax savings and investment returns that could be achieved by collecting earnings sooner against the investment earnings that would be forfeited on the funds used to pay the accelerated income tax liability. Taxpayers should also take into account the potential application of the alternative minimum tax, the phase-out of personal exemptions, and the various limitations on the amount of itemized deductions allowed. Contact your tax adviser to help evaluate the pros and cons of accelerating earnings.

ESTIMATED TAXES

◆ Prior Law

Individual taxpayers are required to pay their anticipated tax liability as it accrues during the current tax year through withholding and/or the payment of estimated tax in quarterly installments. A taxpayer can be penalized for not paying enough tax for a particular installment period. The penalty for underpayment of estimated taxes can be avoided if the total of taxes withheld and estimated tax payments were at least equal to:

1. 100% of the tax reported on the taxpayer's tax return for the prior tax year (an amount commonly called the *100% of last year's tax safe harbor*); or

2. If less, 90% of the current year's actual tax liability.

In either case, the amount arrived at is divided equally among the four installment periods for purposes of determining the amount of each actual quarterly payment of estimated tax.

Individual taxpayers can also use an annualized income approach to avoiding penalties for underpayment of estimated tax.

A *rule of limitation* prohibited certain taxpayers from relying on the 100% of last year's tax safe harbor if their:

1. Adjusted gross income with certain modifications (modified AGI) increased by more than $40,000 ($20,000 for married filing separately) over the prior year; and,

2. Current year modified AGI exceeded $75,000 ($37,500 for married filing separately).

◆ New Law

The *rule of limitation* that prohibited certain tax-payers from utilizing the 100% of last year's tax liability safe harbor is repealed. Under the new law, taxpayers can be certain that there will be no limitation on the 100% of last year's tax safe harbor if their previous year's adjusted gross income is $150,000 or less ($75,000 or less if married filing separately). If their previous year's adjusted gross income exceeds $150,000, a safe harbor is still available, but taxpayers must pay 110% of last year's liability in order to avoid underpayment penalties. Note that the new law retains the rule that taxpayers can avoid penalties for underpayment of tax if at least 90% of their current tax liability is paid through withheld taxes and estimated tax payments.

EXAMPLE: Ms. Green's 1994 income tax liability is $55,000. Her adjusted gross income in 1993 was $175,000, while her 1993 tax liability was $40,000. Ms. Green will avoid an underpayment penalty in 1994 if the total amount of tax withheld and estimated tax payments exceeds 110% of her 1993 tax liability, or $44,000, because her 1993 adjusted gross income exceeded $150,000.

Effective Date

The provision applies to estimated tax payments applicable to tax years beginning after 1993.

Commentary: The *rule of limitation* on the use of the safe harbor was repealed, in part, because it had been widely criticized as forcing affected taxpayers to make often complex and time-consuming predictions of current year tax liabilities in order to calculate appropriate estimated tax installments. On the other hand, all taxpayers whose previous year's adjusted gross income exceeds $150,000 and who plan to rely on the prior year's tax safe harbor to avoid an underpayment penalty must include an extra 10% of their prior year's tax liability in the current year's estimated tax payments.

ALTERNATIVE MINIMUM TAX

◆ Prior Law

Individuals are required to pay an alternative minimum tax (AMT) if it exceeds their regular tax liability. The income amount subject to the AMT is determined by adding back to regular taxable income a number of so-called *preference* items and by making other *adjustments*. These *preferences* and *adjustments* typically reduce regular taxable income and include, for example, itemized deductions such as state and local income and real property taxes and accelerated depreciation claimed on buildings and equipment. The amount arrived at, called *alternative minimum taxable income* (AMTI), is then itself reduced by the exemption amounts shown below, and the balance subjected to a flat 24% AMT rate.

The exemption amounts for each filing status were as follows:

Filing Status	Base Exemption Amount	Less 25% of the Amount by Which AMTI Exceeds
Single/head of household	$30,000	$112,500
Married filing jointly	40,000	150,000
Married filing separately/estate or trust	20,000	75,000

◆ New Law

The AMT rate is raised to 26% on AMTI of $175,000 in excess of the exemption amount, and 28% on AMTI more than $175,000 above the exemption amount. For married taxpayers filing separately, the 28% AMT rate applies to the extent that AMTI is more than $87,500 above the exemption amount. Furthermore, the base exemption amounts are increased by 12.5% to $33,750 for single individuals and heads of household, $45,000 for married taxpayers filing jointly, and $22,500 for married tax-payers filing separately, trusts, and estates.

The new rates are as follows:

Rate	Married Filing Separately	All Other Filers
26%	Up to $87,500 over exemption amount	Up to $175,000 over exemption amount
28%	Greater than $87,500 over exemption amount	Greater than $175,000 over exemption amount

Effective Date

Tax years beginning after December 31, 1992.

Commentary: The table on page 31 compares the minimum amount of preferences and/or adjustments that, when added to selected regular taxable income levels, will subject a taxpayer to AMT liability. It illustrates how the increases in the AMT tax rates and exemption amounts under the new law affect taxpayers who are married and file a joint tax return.

Minimum Dollar Amount of Preferences/ Adjustments to Trigger AMT

Regular Taxable Income	Prior Law	New Law
$50,000	$28,346	$30,396
72,846	32,154	32,154
150,000	42,097	37,628
200,000	43,763	40,369
327,800	64,477	64,477
500,000	114,704	135,818

The table shows that there is no rule of thumb indicating whether taxpayers are better or worse off under the new rates and exemption amounts. Joint filers with regular taxable income of up to $72,846 will be *better off* because of the higher exemption available ($45,000)—that is, they can absorb more AMT adjustments before AMT would apply. At somewhat higher income levels—for example, $150,000 or $200,000 of regular taxable income—it is easier to fall into AMT under the new law. However, joint filers with regular taxable income in excess of $327,800 will be *less* likely to be subject to the AMT—essentially because they will be paying much more in regular tax, given the new higher regular marginal tax rates.

Commentary: To the extent that AMT may be generated by including in AMTI specified itemized deductions, as well as other so-called *exclusion items* such as personal exemptions, tax-exempt interest, and depletion, taxpayers may wish to consider:

- Postponing the payment of such deduction items until a tax year in which the taxpayer will not be exposed to the AMT. These deductions forfeit their tax benefit if they are recognized in a tax year in which the taxpayer owes AMT. Shifting such deductions to non-AMT years can preserve the tax benefit of the deductions.

- Accelerating income until regular tax equals AMT computed with only itemized deductions and other exclusion items taken into account. The accelerated income would be taxed at only a 26% or 28% rate, albeit a year earlier, rather than at tax rates as high as 36% or 39.6%.

AMT EXEMPTION FOR GIFTS OF APPRECIATED PROPERTY

◆ Prior Law

Taxpayers have generally been permitted, in calculating regular taxable income, to deduct the full fair market value of charitable contributions of stock or other property. But in computing the deduction, the fair market value of the donated property was reduced by the amount of ordinary income or short-term capital gain that would have been recognized had the property been sold. However, there was no adjustment in the case of donated long-term capital gain property. For example, if a taxpayer contributed stock worth $10,000 that was purchased more than one year ago for $3,000, the taxpayer would get a $10,000 deduction. The $7,000 gain that had built up would never be recognized.

However, any unrecognized appreciation in donated property was treated as a *preference item* for alternative minimum tax (AMT) purposes. In other words, taxpayers were required to include this appreciation in their alternative minimum taxable income (AMTI) which could, as a result, give rise to AMT. For AMT purposes, the charitable contribution deduction was therefore effectively limited to the taxpayer's cost basis in the property.

Donations made before July 1, 1992, of appreciated tangible personal property that would be used by the charity for its charitable purpose received special treatment. The appreciation built up in such property was not treated as a *preference item* to be added to AMTI. An example of this type of property would be a contribution of paintings to a museum for its collection.

◆ New Law

The treatment of built-in appreciation in donated property as a preference item is eliminated in two stages. First, the special treatment of contributions of tangible personal property, such as paintings and manuscripts, to museums or other charities for their use is extended retroactively from July 1, 1992, and made permanent. Furthermore, tax preference treatment is eliminated for charitable contributions made after December 31, 1992, of *any* type of appreciated property, including, for example, appreciated real property or stock.

> *Commentary 1:* This provision enables taxpayers to recognize a charitable contribution deduction for the full fair market value of appreciated property for *both* regular tax and AMT purposes. Taxpayers who previously made gifts that were not fully deductible due to the regular tax percentage limitations imposed on charitable contributions will still have preference items in future tax years when these carryover amounts ultimately become deductible. Charitable remainder and charitable lead trusts funded with appreciated property now may be even more attractive as planning ideas.

> *Commentary 2*: The Secretary of the Treasury is to establish, not later than one year after the date of enactment, an advance valuation procedure under which a taxpayer can elect to enter into an agreement with the IRS regarding the

value of tangible personal property prior to the donation of such property to a qualifying charitable organization. No such procedure exists under current law. Once in place, it may be advisable to take advantage of the advance valuation procedure for any donation of valuable and/or unusual items, especially in light of the substantial valuation misstatement penalties present in the law.

SUBSTANTIATION REQUIREMENTS FOR CHARITABLE CONTRIBUTIONS

◆ Prior Law

Taxpayers who claim an itemized deduction for charitable contributions are not required to obtain substantiation for claimed charitable contributions from the charities to which contributions were made. If donations of property exceed $500 in any tax year, taxpayers are required to attach Form 8283 to their individual income tax returns to report certain information regarding the contributed property.

Any payment made to a charity is not deductible to the extent that the taxpayer received some benefit in return. For example, payment for a charity dinner would only be deductible to the extent it exceeded the value of the dinner itself.

Tax-exempt organizations eligible to receive deductible contributions are not required to state explicitly whether contributions are deductible or whether all or part of a contribution should be offset by goods or services furnished to the donor.

◆ New Law

Taxpayers must now obtain a contemporaneous written acknowledgment from any charitable organization to which a contribution of $250 or more is made in order to deduct that contribution. *Contemporaneous* for this purpose means that the written acknowledgment must be obtained by the taxpayer on or before the earlier of the date on which the return is actually filed for the year in which the contribution was made or the due date for the return, including extensions. A canceled check does not constitute adequate substantiation for a contribution of money. The written acknowledgment must state the amount of cash and a description (but not value) of any property other than cash contributed. It must also state whether the charitable organization provided any goods or services in consideration, in whole or in part, for the contribution and, if so, a description and good faith estimate of the value of goods or services provided. If the goods or services provided as consideration for the contribution consist solely of *intangible religious benefits*, a statement to that effect must be included in the written acknowledgment.

Taxpayers are not required to obtain substantiation for a donation if the charitable organization files a return with the IRS which includes the same information otherwise required from the taxpayer. Note, however, that primary responsibility lies with the taxpayer, not the charitable organization, to request and maintain in his or her records the required substantiation.

Furthermore, for any *quid pro quo contribution* over $75 (that is, any contribution for which the charity provides goods or services such as a charity dinner) the charity must provide a statement to the donor that reports the estimated value of the goods or services received by the donor in exchange for the contribution. As under prior law, a payment to a charity is deductible only to the extent that it exceeds the value of any goods or services received in return.

Effective Date

Contributions made after December 31, 1993.

EXAMPLE 1: Dr. Porter contributes property with a value of $300 to charity. He must obtain a receipt describing the donated property and indicating whether any goods or services were received in exchange. If the charity provided goods or services, the receipt or acknowledgment must contain a good faith estimate of the value of the goods or service. However, the charity does not have to value the property it received from Dr. Porter.

EXAMPLE 2: A charity receives a $200 contribution in exchange for which the donor, Mr. Smith, receives a dinner valued at $50. The charity must inform Mr. Smith in writing that only $150 is deductible as a charitable contribution.

> *Commentary:* In general, separate payments are not combined for purposes of the substantiation requirement, so a taxpayer could deduct separate contributions of less than $250 from each paycheck or make monthly payments to a charity without running afoul of the requirement. However, a taxpayer could not, for example, simply write multiple checks on the same day in order to avoid substantiation. Similarly, separate payments made at different times with respect to different fundraising events are not aggregated to determine whether the charity must inform the donor of the value of any benefit received in return for a donation in excess of $75.

ESTATE AND GIFT TAX RATES

◆ Prior Law

The federal gift and estate taxes are unified so that a single progressive tax rate schedule is applied to an individual's cumulative gifts and bequests. For decedents dying or gifts made after 1992, the estate and gift marginal tax rates ranged from 18% to 50% for cumulative gifts and bequests larger than $2.5 million. Prior to 1993, the top tax rate was 55%. In addition, the tax benefit of the graduated rates and the unified estate and gift tax credit available to each individual of $192,800 were phased out by imposing a 5% tax on cumulative gifts and bequests between $10 million and $18,340,000.

◆ New Law

The new law restores the top marginal tax rates that were in effect before 1993. Specifically, for taxable transfers between $2.5 million and $3.0 million, the tax rate is 53%. For taxable transfers over $3.0 million, the top tax rate is 55%. The 5% surtax range applies to taxable transfers between $10 million and $21,040,000. This phase-out means that a taxable estate of $21,040,000 or more pays tax at a rate of 55% on *every* dollar included in the taxable estate.

Note that the flat tax imposed on generation-skipping transfers is also restored to 55%.

Effective Date

The provision is effective for decedents dying, gifts made, and generation skipping transfers occurring after 1992.

Commentary: With the reinstatement of the 53% and 55% brackets, a $3 million estate would owe $15,000 more in estate taxes, while a $5 million estate would pay $115,000 more.

REPEAL OF LUXURY EXCISE TAX ON BOATS, AIRCRAFT, JEWELRY, AND FURS

◆ Prior Law

An excise tax was imposed on the first retail sale or use of certain luxury items. The tax equaled 10% of the excess of the retail sales price over the following threshold amounts:

Item	*Threshold*
Automobiles, light trucks and vans (other than taxicabs)	$30,000
Boats (if not used exclusively in a qualifying trade or business)	$100,000
Aircraft (if not used at least 80% in a trade or business)	$250,000
Jewelry and furs	$10,000

The tax did not apply to wholesale sales or to subsequent sales of used items, such as antique jewelry pieces. Also, if a customer returned an item for a full refund, the tax was also refunded.

◆ New Law

The luxury tax imposed on boats, airplanes, jewelry, and furs is repealed.

The $30,000 threshold for the luxury tax on automobiles is indexed annually for inflation occurring after 1990 (each annual adjustment is rounded down to the nearest increment of $2,000). Consequently, the threshold for automobiles purchased from the date the new law was enacted through the end of 1993 is $32,000. Cars purchased by automobile dealers for use as demonstrators and specialty equipment installed on a passenger vehicle for use by disabled individuals are exempt from the luxury tax.

Effective Date

These provisions generally apply to retail sales occurring after 1992 and to passenger vehicles purchased after August 10, 1993. The exemption for accessories or modifications purchased by disabled persons is retroactively effective for sales after 1990.

Commentary: Taxpayers are entitled to a refund of any luxury tax previously paid that has now been retroactively eliminated. Affected taxpayers may request a refund from the seller from whom the taxed item was purchased. The seller then files either for a refund on Form 843 or for a credit on Form 720.

HEALTH INSURANCE DEDUCTION FOR SELF-EMPLOYED INDIVIDUALS

◆ Prior Law

Until the provision expired on June 30, 1992, self-employed individuals and owners of 2% or more of the stock in an S corporation could generally deduct (as an adjustment to gross income) 25% of the premiums paid for health insurance coverage of the individual and his or her spouse and dependents. The deduction was not allowed if the individual or his or her spouse was eligible for employer-paid health insurance.

◆ New Law

The deduction is retroactively reinstated for premiums paid for coverage from July 1, 1992, through December 31, 1993. In addition, the determination of whether a self-employed individual or his or her spouse is eligible for employer-paid health insurance benefits is made on a monthly basis rather than on an annual basis.

Effective Date

Tax years ending after June 30, 1992.

> *Commentary:* To the extent that taxpayers have already filed income tax returns treating the deduction as having expired on June 30, 1992, they may wish to file amended returns reflecting the reinstatement of the deduction. This deduction may be extended further if a health care reform bill is passed by Congress. If not, Congress will once again need to enact other legislation to extend the health insurance deduction for self-employed individuals.

CAPITAL GAINS INCENTIVE FOR INVESTMENT IN SMALL BUSINESS

◆ Prior Law

The gain from the sale of stock of a corporation held for more than one year generally is treated as a long-term capital gain. Gain from the sale of stock held for less time is a short-term capital gain. A taxpayer's net capital gain is the amount by which the taxpayer's net long-term capital gains exceed net short-term capital losses. For an individual, net capital gains are taxed at the same rates as the individual's ordinary income, except that the top rate for capital gains is 28%.

◆ New Law

The Act provides that a noncorporate taxpayer who holds *qualified small business stock* (QSBS) for more than five years can exclude from gross income 50% of any gain realized from the sale or exchange of the stock. This exclusion is limited to the greater of:

1. 10 times the taxpayer's basis in the stock; or

2. $10 million in gain from all of the taxpayer's transactions in stock of that corporation (held for more than five years).

EXAMPLE: Assume Taxpayer purchases 1000 shares of newly-issued X Corporation's QSBS for $6 million, at the beginning of Year 1. In Year 6, Taxpayer sells 500 shares of X Corporation's QSBS at a $4 million gain. Taxpayer excludes $2 million of gain from the sale from gross income in Year 6. In Year 7, Taxpayer sells 300 more shares of X Corporation's QSBS at a gain of $20 million. Taxpayer may only exclude $8 million in gain from gross income in Year 7. Taxpayer's Year 7 exclusion is limited to $8 million because the total exclusion from gross income attributable to one corporation's QSBS is limited to $10 million.

The rules for determining whether stock is QSBS can be summarized as follows:

- The stock must be newly issued stock.

- The stock cannot be acquired in exchange for other stock.

- The issuing corporation must be a C corporation, but may not be a cooperative, Domestic International Sales Corporation (DISC), former DISC, Real Estate Investment Trust (REIT), Regulated Investment Company (RIC), Real Estate Mortgage Investment Conduit (REMIC), a corporation having a possessions tax credit election in effect, or owning a subsidiary who has a possessions tax credit election in effect.

- At least 80% of the corporation's assets must be used in the active conduct of a *qualified trade or business*, or in the start-up of a future *qualified trade or business*.

- A qualified trade or business is any business other than one involving the performance of services in the fields of health, law, engineering, architecture, accounting, actuarial science, performing arts, consulting, athletics, financial services, brokerage services, or any other trade or business where the principal asset of the business is the reputation or skill of one or more employees. A qualified trade or business also cannot involve the businesses of banking, insurance, financing, leasing, investing, or similar businesses, farming, or certain businesses involving natural resource extraction or production, and businesses operating a hotel, motel, restaurant, or similar business.

- The corporation may not have greater than $50 million in gross assets (i.e., sum of cash plus the aggregate fair market value of other corporate property) at the time the qualified small business stock is issued. If the corporation meets this test at the time of issuance of the stock, a subsequent event that violates this rule will not disqualify stock that previously qualified.

A special anti-abuse rule is provided to keep a large corporation from putting assets in a subsidiary so that the contributing corporation can be treated as a QSBS.

With some limitations, if the QSBS is owned by a partnership (or certain other pass-through entities), the benefit of the exclusion from gross income may inure to the partners (or others with an ownership interest in the pass-through entity). However, the partner (or other owner) must have been a partner (or owner) in the partnership (or entity) at the time the partnership (or entity) acquired the QSBS and at all times until the QSBS is transferred by the partnership (or entity).

Any capital gain excluded under the new rules is not taken into account in computing a taxpayer's long-term capital gains or in reducing the taxpayer's capital losses. The taxable portion of the gain from the sale of QSBS is taxed at a maximum tax rate of 28%. However, one-half of the gain excluded from gross income under the new rules is treated as an item of tax preference for purposes of the alternative minimum tax, and therefore will have to be added to a taxpayer's taxable income in computing the taxpayer's alternative minimum tax.

Effective Date

The new rules apply to stock issued after August 10, 1993.

> *Commentary 1:* The lawmakers who have supported the new capital gains provision believe that by targeting the provision to smaller businesses it will provide more effective incentives for long-term equity investments in those businesses. By limiting the preferential capital gains treatment to stock that is newly issued, the provision is designed to respond to concerns that an across-the-board capital gains provision would provide a windfall to wealthy investors who already own appreciated investments.

> *Commentary 2:* This new provision could benefit the shareholders of corporations that are engaged in retail sales, manufacturing, or production of high-technology products.

> *Commentary 3:* Start-up companies are routinely faced with the question of when their trade or business begins. This provision eases such determinations by permitting assets used in certain start-up activities, research and experimental activities or in-house research activities, to be treated as used in an active conduct

of a qualified trade or business for purposes of the 80% test described above.

Note: A new provision has also been added which provides that, under certain circumstances, gain on the sale of publicly traded securities will not be recognized (i.e., taxed) if the proceeds from the sale are used to acquire common stock in a *specialized small business investment company* (SSBIC) within a 60-day period. (See, *Rollover of Gain From Sale of Publicly Traded Securities Into Specialized Small Business Investment Companies* below.) Normally, the basis of the SSBIC stock acquired must be reduced by the amount of the gain that is not recognized. If an individual acquires QSBS in a corporation that is a SSBIC in order to take advantage of this nonrecognition provision, the basis of the QSBS is not required to be reduced by the amount of the gain not recognized.

ROLLOVER OF GAIN FROM SALE OF PUBLICLY TRADED SECURITIES INTO SPECIALIZED SMALL BUSINESS INVESTMENT COMPANIES

◆ Prior Law

Recognition of gain or loss is generally required in transactions where the taxpayer has sold, exchanged, or disposed of publicly traded securities.

◆ New Law

Congress believed that small businesses have a difficult time attracting capital and needed legislation that would permit corporations and individuals to roll over the gain from the sale of publicly traded securities into the purchase of common stock or a partnership interest in an investment company whose purpose was to provide small business companies with working capital. Corporations and individuals can elect to roll over, without the payment of any capital gain tax, the capital gain from the sale of publicly traded securities (defined as stock or debt traded on an established securities market) into the purchase of common stock or a partnership interest in a specialized small business investment company (SSBIC). An SSBIC must be a licensed partnership or corporation under the Small Business Administration's Small Business Investment Act of 1958, §301(d).

The rollover must occur within 60 days from the sale date of the securities. Should the proceeds from the securities sale exceed the cost of purchasing the interest in the SSBIC, the taxpayer is required to currently recognize such excess gain in income. The taxpayer's basis in the SSBIC common stock or partnership interest is reduced by the amount of any gain that is not currently recognized on the securities sale. The basis in the SSBIC common stock is not reduced, however, for purposes of calculating the gain eligible for the 50% exclusion for qualified small business stock under new §1202.

Not all taxpayers are eligible to roll over their gain from the sale of publicly traded securities. Partnerships, S corporations, trusts and estates cannot make this election. Additionally, the amount of gain that an individual may elect to roll over, for any tax year, is limited to the lesser of $50,000 or $500,000 reduced by any gain previously excluded under this provision. For corporations, these limits are $250,000 and $1,000,000. The individual limits apply to a husband and wife filing a joint return, and the corporate limits apply to a consolidated group of filers.

EXAMPLE: An individual or corporation presently holds a portfolio of publicly traded stock. The sale of the stock will trigger capital gains for the taxpayer. Under this provision, the stockholder would be able to rollover the capital gain, tax-free, if the taxpayer uses the entire proceeds from the sale to purchase common stock or a partnership interest in a SSBIC within 60 days from the date it sold the stock.

Effective Date

The provision applies to sales of publicly traded securities occurring on or after the date of enactment.

2

◆ ◆ ◆ ◆ ◆ ◆ ◆

CHANGES OF CONCERN TO BUSINESS IN GENERAL

CORPORATE TAX RATES

◆ Prior Law

The taxable income of a corporation was taxed at three rates ranging from 15% (on the first $50,000 of taxable income) to 34% (on taxable income in excess of $75,000).

Taxable Income	Tax Rate
Up to $50,000	15%
$50,001–$75,000	25%
$75,001–$100,000	34%
Over $100,000	34%[1*]

* (see footnote on following page)

◆ New Law

The rates of tax on corporate taxable income are as follows:

Taxable Income	Tax Rate
Up to $50,000	15%
$50,001–$75,000	25%
$75,001–$10 million	34%[2]
Over $10 million	35%[3]

(1) Taxpayers with taxable income between $75,001 and $100,000 paid a 34% rate. An additional 5% tax not to exceed $11,750 was imposed on corporate taxable income over $100,000, up to $335,000. This increase in tax phased out the benefits of the 15% and 25% rates. Therefore, corporations with taxable income over $335,000 paid a flat rate of 34%.

(2) The phase-out of the benefits of the 15% and 25% rates still applies. Thus, taxpayers with taxable income between $75,001 and $100,000 still pay a 34% rate, and an additional 5% tax not to exceed $11,750 is imposed on corporate taxable income over $100,000, up to $335,000.

(3) An additional 3% tax not to exceed $100,000 is imposed on corporate taxable income over $15 million. This increase in tax phases out the benefits of the 34% rate. Therefore, corporations with taxable income over $18.333 million pay a flat rate of 35%.

The income tax rate for personal service corporations and the maximum capital gain rate for corporations have been increased from 34% to 35%.

Effective Date

The new rates apply to tax years beginning on or after January 1, 1993. A fiscal year corporation is required to use a blend of the old and new rates for a tax year that includes but does not begin on January 1, 1993. Accordingly, the corporation's applicable tax rate will be a weighted average of the rates.

Penalties for the underpayment of estimated taxes are waived for underpayments attributable solely to the changes in tax rates.

A fiscal year taxpayer, who is required to use a blend of the old and new rates for a tax year that includes but does not begin on January 1, 1993 (e.g., a January 31, 1993 year end), and that may have filed or extended a tax return, will be required to pay the additional tax imposed. However, for purposes of determining whether a valid extension exists, taxpayers are required to remit the estimated unpaid tax liability with the extension request. The determination of the required amount will be made under prior law.

Commentary 1: In addition to the cash flow impact of increased corporate tax rates, there may be a financial statement impact under Statement of Financial Accounting Standards

No. 109, *Accounting for Income Taxes* (FAS 109). Under FAS 109, deferred tax assets or liabilities are measured using the enacted tax rates expected to apply to taxable income in the period in which the deferred tax asset or liability is expected to be settled or realized. In cases where there has been a change in the tax rate or laws, the balance sheet is adjusted for the effect of the change. This change is recorded as a component of income tax expense relating to continuing operations in the period in which the law is enacted. For some companies, the increase in the corporate tax rate to 35% may result in a higher tax provision due to the adjustment of the deferred taxes.

EXAMPLE: A company has net deferred tax liabilities of $340,000 at the beginning of the year, applying a 34% rate. During the year, assume the company has no change in its temporary differences, but the tax rate increases to 35%. Under FAS 109, deferred tax liabilities would be adjusted to $350,000. The $10,000 difference reflects the rate change that will flow through the tax provision as a component of income tax expense, thereby reducing net income for financial statement purposes.

Commentary 2: As rates increase, the incentive for accelerating deductions increases. Thus, techniques used to accelerate deductions and defer income should provide greater benefits in the future.

Commentary 3: The corporate alternative minimum tax (AMT) rate has not changed and remains at 20%. Since the spread between the AMT rate and the top regular tax rate increased by one percentage point, certain taxpayers may be able to further benefit by taking certain deductions which otherwise would be included in AMTI, such as accelerated depreciation or utilization of certain credits, without paying AMT.

ACCUMULATED EARNINGS AND PERSONAL HOLDING COMPANY TAXES

◆ Prior Law

The accumulated earnings tax (AET) is a penalty tax imposed on C corporations that accumulate earnings beyond reasonable business needs. There is a presumption that such accumulations are made to avoid the imposition of a second level of tax on the earnings of a C corporation when the earnings are distributed to the shareholders (e.g., the income tax paid by an individual shareholder on dividends received from a corporation). Reasonable business needs include working capital and funds for expansion and diversification. The AET is imposed on an amount denominated *accumulated taxable income*, which consists of taxable income with certain adjustments, reductions, and an accumulated earnings credit. The AET rate was 28%.

The personal holding company (PHC) tax was also imposed at 28% on undistributed earnings of certain closely held companies with largely passive investments or personal service income.

◆ New Law

The AET and PHC tax rates are increased to 39.6%.

Effective Date

The new rates apply for tax years beginning after December 31, 1992.

> *Commentary:* The 11.6 percentage point rate increase underscores the importance of establishing and documenting reasonable business needs, including working capital needs, in order to avoid the application of the accumulated earnings penalty tax. The AET has taken on added significance as the IRS has made it a hot issue in audits of public companies in recent years.

CORPORATE ESTIMATED TAXES

◆ Prior Law

For tax years beginning before January 1, 1997, to avoid penalties for underpayment of estimated taxes, a corporation was required to make quarterly estimated tax payments that totaled at least 97% of the tax liability shown on the corporation's return for the current tax year. A corporation may estimate its tax liability for the current year by annualizing its income through the period ending with either the month or the quarter ending prior to the estimated payment due date. For tax years beginning after December 31, 1996, the 97% requirement would have become a 91% requirement.

Under a safe harbor rule, any corporation that is not a *large corporation* may still avoid penalties for underpayment if it makes four timely estimated tax payments each equal to at least 25% of the tax liability shown on its return for the preceding tax year (otherwise known as the *prior year tax exception*). A *large corporation* may also use this rule with respect to its estimated tax payment but only for the first quarter of its current tax year. A *large corporation* is one that had taxable income of $1 million or more for any of the three preceding tax years.

◆ New Law

A corporation that does not or may not use the prior year tax exception is required to base its estimated tax payments on 100% of the tax shown on its return for the current year. The amount required to be paid per installment is as follows:

| | % of Tax Due | |
Installment	Prior Law	New Law
1	24.25	25
2	48.50	50
3	72.75	75
4	97.00	100

There is no change to the *prior year exception* (safe harbor) for either small or large corporations, but the income annualization methods used to determine estimated tax payments have been modified. First, there is a new set of periods over which a corporation may elect to annualize income. Thus, there are now three alternative sets of periods a corporation may use to annualize income. Second, corporations are required to annually elect which of the three alternative periods they will use.

Specifically, annualized income is determined based upon the following:

Method 1

Installment	Periods for Applying Annualization
1	First 3 months of the tax year [1]
2	First 3 months of the tax year
3	First 6 months of the tax year
4	First 9 months of the tax year

Method 2

Installment	Periods for Applying Annualization
1	First 2 months of the tax year [1]
2	First 4 months of the tax year
3	First 7 months of the tax year
4	First 10 months of the tax year

Method 3

Installment	Periods for Applying Annualization
1	First 3 months of the tax year [1]
2	First 5 months of the tax year
3	First 8 months of the tax year
4	First 11 months of the tax year

(1) Note: A large corporation may use the *prior year tax exception* by paying at least 25% of the prior year tax.

An election to use either of the alternative methods previously described must be made on or before the due date of the first estimated tax installment for the tax year for which the election is to apply, in a manner prescribed by the Secretary of the Treasury.

Effective Date

These rules apply to tax years beginning after December 31, 1993.

> *Commentary:* Once an annualized method is adopted for a tax year, a taxpayer cannot change the method for the remainder of the year. Thus, taxpayers should anticipate when income will be earned during the year and elect a method that defers recognition of such income to later quarters in order to defer cash payments until the end of the year. For example, if a calendar year company earns most of its income at the end of each quarter (i.e., March, June, September and December) Method 2 or Method 3 would require less cash to be paid for estimated tax payments than Method 1. However, a larger amount would be due with the tax return or extension.

ALTERNATIVE MINIMUM TAX RELIEF

◆ Prior Law

A corporate taxpayer is subject to an alternative minimum tax (AMT) to the extent that the taxpayer's tentative minimum tax exceeds its regular income tax liability. For a corporation, the tentative minimum tax generally equals 20% of the excess of the corporation's alternative minimum taxable income (AMTI) over an exemption amount. AMTI is the corporation's taxable income modified by certain adjustments and increased by certain tax preference items (e.g., certain tax-exempt interest).

One of the adjustments made to taxable income in computing AMTI relates to depreciation. For AMT purposes, unless the taxpayer has elected to use the straight-line method for regular tax purposes, depreciation on most personal property to which the Modified Accelerated Cost Recovery System (MACRS) applies is computed using the 150% declining balance method (switching to straight line in the year necessary to maximize the deduction) over the property's class life.

For tax years beginning after 1989, the AMTI of a corporation is increased by an amount equal to 75% of the amount by which adjusted current earnings (ACE) exceeds AMTI (as determined without this adjustment). Generally, ACE equals AMTI with additional adjustments that generally follow the rules used by corporations in computing earnings and profits. For ACE purposes, depreciation was computed using the straight-line method over the class life of the property. Thus, a corporation that uses MACRS for regular tax purposes generally had to make two additional depreciation computations for purposes of AMT.

◆ New Law

The Act eliminates the depreciation component of the ACE adjustment. As under prior law, unless the straight-line method was used for regular tax purposes, corporations will compute depreciation for MACRS tangible personal property for AMT purposes by using the 150% declining balance method over the class life of the property.

Effective Date

This rule is effective for property placed in service after December 31, 1993.

Commentary: While this change should simplify the calculation of depreciation for alternative minimum tax purposes, taxpayers must continue to make the ACE adjustment for depreciation for property placed in service before January 1, 1994.

MOVING EXPENSE DEDUCTION

◆ Prior Law

Individuals are permitted to take an itemized deduction for moving expenses incurred in connection with a new work location. Under prior law, in addition to the expense of transporting the taxpayer (and members of the taxpayer's household), and household goods and personal effects of the new residence, deductible moving expenses included expenses incurred on house-hunting trips, temporary living expenses for up to 30 days, and expenses incident to the sale, purchase, or lease of a new residence and/or to settling an unexpired lease on the old residence.

One limitation that applied to the moving expense deduction was that the individual's new principal place of work had to be at least 35 miles farther from the taxpayer's former residence than was his or her former principal place of work.

◆ New Law

Deductible moving expenses only include the expense of transporting the taxpayer (and members of the taxpayer's household) to the new residence, as well as the cost of moving household goods and personal effects. Deductible moving expenses no longer include the following:

- the cost of meals;

- the cost of pre-move house-hunting trips;

- the cost of temporary living expenses;

- the costs incident to the sale or lease of the old residence, including settling of an unexpired lease, and;

- the costs incident to the purchase or lease of a new residence.

In addition, the individual's new principal place of work must be at least 50 miles farther from the former residence than was his or her former principal place of work. Expenses that qualify as moving expenses that are not paid or reimbursed by the taxpayer's employer are allowable as a deduction in calculating adjusted gross income (AGI). Thus, moving expenses are no longer deducted as an itemized deduction. Moving expenses paid or reimbursed by the employer are excludable from gross income of the employee, and are not included in the employee's Form W-2.

Effective Date

These rules apply to moving expenses paid or incurred after December 31, 1993.

Commentary: If you are planning to move as a result of employment, you may want to pay or incur as many of these moving expenses as possible by December 31, 1993. For example:

- if you need to look for a new residence, travel before December 31, 1993 so that the meals consumed while traveling and the cost of the house-hunting trip are deductible;

- if you know in advance that you need to settle an unexpired lease of the old residence, be sure to settle the costs by December 31, 1993; and

- try to sell your old residence and purchase your new residence by December 31, 1993, so that the costs incident to the sale or purchase are deductible.

BUSINESS MEALS AND ENTERTAINMENT

◆ Prior Law

Meals and entertainment expenses incurred for business or investment purposes are deductible if certain legal and substantiation requirements are met. No deduction is allowed, however, for meal or beverage expenses that are lavish or extravagant under the circumstances. Under prior law, the amount of the deduction generally was limited to 80% of the expense that met these requirements.

◆ New Law

The deductible portion of business meals and entertainment expenses is limited to 50%.

Effective Date

These rules apply to tax years beginning after December 31, 1993.

EMPLOYER TAX CREDIT FOR FICA TAXES ON TIP INCOME

◆ Prior Law

All income earned by an employee from gratuities (tip income) is treated as wages paid by the employee's employer for purposes of the Federal Insurance Contributions Act (FICA). Thus, an employer must pay the FICA tax (which is often referred to as the social security tax) on the tip income of its employees. This FICA tax rate is 7.65%. Employers are allowed a business deduction for this expense.

For purposes of the minimum wage requirements, an employee's tip income is treated as a wage paid by the employer, to the extent of 50% of the minimum wage.

◆ New Law

A new tax credit is provided for employers that provide food or beverage services to customers at the employer's place of business, where employees are customarily given tips by customers for food or beverage services. The credit is equal to an employer's FICA tax liability on the tip income of its employees, less the amount of the tip income used to satisfy the minimum wage requirements. The employer may not take a deduction for that portion of the FICA tax that is used as a tax credit.

This credit is part of the employer's general business tax credit. However, any credits that are not used in a tax year may not be carried back to a tax year ending before the date of enactment of the Act.

Effective Date

The new credit is available for FICA taxes paid after December 31, 1993.

> *Commentary:* The following example illustrates the computation of this credit. Taxpayer owns and operates a restaurant business. Employee is employed part-time as a waiter in Taxpayer's restaurant. During Taxpayer's tax year ending December 31, Taxpayer paid Employee $2,000 dollars in hourly wages. If Taxpayer had paid Employee the minimum wage, Employee's hourly wages would have been $2,125. In the

same year, Employee also received $4,000 in tip income while working in the restaurant. Of this amount, $125 ($2,125 − $2,000) was used to satisfy the minimum wage requirement. Thus, Taxpayer was required to pay the FICA tax on $6,000 of Employee's total *wages*. The total FICA tax paid by Taxpayer was $459 ($6,000 × 7.65%). Taxpayer's tax credit is equal to the FICA tax paid on Employee's tip income not used to satisfy the minimum wage requirements (i.e., $296 ($4,000 − $125) × 7.65%). Taxpayer may not deduct this $296 of FICA tax.

CLUB DUES

◆ Prior Law

A deduction was permitted for club dues if the taxpayer established that the use of the club was primarily for the furtherance of the taxpayer's trade or business and the specific expense was directly related to the active conduct of that trade or business. No deduction was permitted for an initiation or similar fee that is payable only upon joining a club if the useful life of the fee extended over more than one year.

◆ New Law

No deduction is allowed for club dues. This rule applies to all types of clubs, including business, social, athletic, luncheon, sporting, hotel, and airport clubs. Specific business expenses, such as meals and entertainment that may occur at a club would be deductible to the extent that they otherwise satisfy the standard for deductibility.

Effective Date

This rule applies to club dues paid or incurred after December 31, 1993.

> *Commentary:* Taxpayers may consider prepaying certain club dues by December 31, 1993. However, there are limitations on the extent to which a prepaid expense can be deducted. For example, under similar circumstances when the Tax Reform Act of 1986 was passed, the IRS limited deductions for an individual's prepaid miscellaneous business and investment expenses. If an individual makes a payment in the current year as a prepayment for several years of expense, the IRS may only allow a deduction for the portion of the payment that relates to the year immediately following the tax year in which the payment is made.

LOBBYING EXPENSE DEDUCTION

◆ Prior Law

Under prior law, a taxpayer could deduct ordinary and necessary expenses paid or incurred in carrying on a trade or business for activities directly related to appearances before or communications with legislative bodies, or their members, concerning legislation of direct interest to the taxpayer and similar amounts paid to communicate information concerning legislation between the taxpayer and organizations of which the taxpayer was a member. The taxpayer could also deduct that portion of dues paid or incurred to an organization to which the taxpayer belonged that were attributable to the activities described above. No deduction was allowed for amounts paid or incurred for participation or intervention in a political campaign on behalf of a candidate for public office (campaign expenses) or for attempts to influence the general public, or segments thereof, with respect to legislative matters, elections, or referendums (grass roots lobbying expenses). In addition, no deduction was allowed for lobbying of foreign governments.

◆ New Law

The Act retains the prior rules denying deductions for campaign expenses, grass roots lobbying expenses, and foreign lobbying. The Act adds new rules that disallow deductions for certain other lobbying expenses. The new rules disallow deduction for the costs of any attempt to influence state or Federal legislation and any communications with a *covered executive branch official* in an attempt to influence official actions or positions of that official. Covered executive branch officials include the President, Vice President, certain White House officials, cabinet level officials, the two most senior officials in each Executive agency, and certain other officials. The new rules apply to attempts to influence legislation through communications with both members or employees of a legislative body and other government officials who participate in the formulation of legislation. The rules apply to costs for research for, or preparation, planning, or coordination of such lobbying activities.

The ordinary and necessary business expenses of those in the business of lobbying on behalf of others are exempted from the new disallowance rules. If a taxpayer has de minimis amounts ($2,000 or less) of in-house lobbying expenses (not counting payments to a professional lobbying organization or organization dues allocable to lobbying activities), those in-house expenses are exempt from the general disallowance, and may be deductible business expenses.

The costs of attempting to influence legislation at the level of a political subdivision of a state (e.g., a county or municipality) are deductible under rules identical to those contained in the prior law.

The new rules also disallow business deductions for dues or contributions to an exempt organization other than a charity (e.g., a trade association), to the extent those payments are allocable to the lobbying costs of the exempt organization. To implement this rule, a new reporting requirement is placed on such exempt organizations, to inform their members or contributors (and the IRS) of the portion of their dues or contributions that are disallowed under this rule. However, an exempt organization can avoid the reporting requirements if the organization:

- has de minimis ($2,000 or less) in-house lobbying expenses and makes no payments to third parties for lobbying services;

- pays a so-called *proxy* tax on the total amount of its lobbying expenditures (up to the amount of the dues it receives) at the highest corporate marginal rate, to offset the deductions of its members that would have been disallowed if the organization had informed the members;[1] or

- can show that at least 90% of its dues or contributions come from members who cannot otherwise take a deduction for their payments to the organization.

---

[1] Under such circumstances, a portion of the member's dues will be nondeductible.

In general, no similar disallowance applies to deductions for payments to charitable exempt organizations (e.g., tax-exempt hospitals) unless the charity lobbies on issues that have a direct financial impact on the donor's trade or business and the donor made the contribution to receive a deduction for otherwise nondeductible lobbying costs.

Effective Date

This rule applies to amounts paid or incurred after December 31, 1993.

> *Commentary:* There are a number of contacts with the government that should not be considered lobbying contacts, including (but not limited to) those compelled by subpoena, statute, regulation, etc.; those made in response to public notices soliciting communications to the public; those made to a Federal official with regard to judicial proceedings, criminal or civil law enforcement inquiries, investigations, or proceedings. Congress has expressed an intent that such contacts should not be considered lobbying. Thus, expenses incurred in dealing with the IRS and Treasury Department on matters involving private letter rulings, technical advice memoranda, and regulation commentary would remain deductible.

TRAVEL EXPENSES FOR SPOUSES, DEPENDENTS, AND OTHER INDIVIDUALS

◆ Prior Law

Generally, expenses for travel conducted in carrying on a trade or business, or for the production of income are deductible as a business expense. If an individual's spouse or other family member accompanied him or her on a business trip, travel expenses attributable to the spouse or other family member were deductible only if the individual adequately showed that the presence of the spouse or other family member on the trip had a bona fide business purpose. The performance of some incidental service by the spouse or other family member did not cause the expenses to qualify as deductible business expenses.

◆ New Law

A deduction is allowed for travel expenses paid or incurred with respect to a spouse, dependent, or other individual accompanying a person on business travel **only** if the spouse, dependent, or other individual is a bona fide employee of the person paying or reimbursing the expenses and the following apply.

- The travel of the spouse, dependent, or other individual is for a bona fide business purpose.

- The expenses incurred would otherwise be deductible.

This rule does not apply to travel expenses for spouses, dependents, and other individuals that otherwise qualify as deductible moving expenses.

Effective Date

This rule applies to expenses paid or incurred after December 31, 1993.

EXAMPLE: Mrs. X, an employee of Taxpayer, is accompanied on a business trip by her husband Mr. X, who is not an employee of Taxpayer. Because Mr. X assisted his wife on the trip by entertaining clients, helping her conduct a seminar, and performing other substantial business services, Mr. X's presence on the trip had a bona fide business purpose. Taxpayer paid all of Mrs. and Mr. X's travel expenses. Under the prior law, Taxpayer may have been able to deduct the costs of Mrs. and Mr. X's travel as an ordinary and necessary business expense. Under the new law, Taxpayer may not deduct the costs of Mr. X's travel because he is not an employee of Taxpayer.

In order to qualify, a person must be a bona fide employee. However, there is no definition of bona fide employee or bona fide business purpose contained in the Statute. Thus, whether a bona fide employee or bona fide business purpose exists will be determined on a case-by-case basis.

EXTENSION OF RESEARCH AND DEVELOPMENT CREDIT

◆ Prior Law

A 20% tax credit (the *research credit*) was available if a taxpayer increased its qualified research expenses in the current tax year over a base amount. Generally, the base amount was the product of a taxpayer's fixed-base percentage and the taxpayer's average annual gross receipts for the four years preceding the current tax year. The fixed-base percentage was a ratio of the taxpayer's qualified research expenses to its gross receipts during the period 1984-1988 (the *fixed-base period*). A taxpayer that did not have both qualified research expenses and gross receipts in at least three years during the fixed base period (a *start-up company*) would be assigned a fixed-base percentage of .03 (or 3%). Expenses paid or incurred after June 30, 1992, were not eligible for the research credit.

◆ New Law

The prior rules governing the research credit are extended (retroactively) for an additional 3 years.

In addition, there is a new rule regarding the determination of the fixed-base percentage for start-up companies. A start-up company is assigned a fixed-base percentage of .03 for each of its first five tax years after 1993 in which it incurs qualified research expenses. For subsequent tax years, the fixed-base percentage will be computed based on its actual levels of research spending.

Effective Date

The research credit may be computed using qualified research expenses paid or incurred before July 1, 1995.

> *Commentary:* Since the enactment of the research credit in 1981, the definition of qualified research has always been based, in part, on the definition of deductible research or experimental expenditures in §174 of the Internal Revenue Code. As part of the Tax Reform Act of 1986, Congress modified the definition of qualified research by making it more restrictive for purposes of the research credit. In the Conference Report to this Act, the Conferees affirmed the congressional intent that neither the enactment of the research credit in 1981, nor the modifications to the credit provisions in 1986, affect the definition of *research or experimental expenditures* for purposes of the deduction provided in §174. Thus, because the definitions of the terms *research or experimen-*

tal (for the deduction) and *qualified research* (for the credit) are not identical, certain research and development costs incurred by taxpayers may be deductible, even though such costs do not qualify for the research credit.

In March 1993, the Internal Revenue Service issued proposed regulations clarifying what activities constitute qualified research. Since the research credit has been extended retroactively, taxpayers should evaluate their research activities using this revised definition to insure that they are receiving the maximum benefit from this tax credit.

SMALL BUSINESS EQUIPMENT EXPENSING ELECTION

◆ Prior Law

A taxpayer that annually purchases sufficiently small dollar amounts of certain types of depreciable property, known as *§179 property*, may elect to deduct a portion of the cost of the §179 property. Generally, §179 property is depreciable tangible personal property used in the active conduct of a trade or business. Under prior law, a taxpayer could deduct up to $10,000 of §179 property costs. However, the deduction may not exceed the taxpayer's taxable income derived from the trade or business for the tax year. Any amount of deduction not allowed by this limitation may be carried forward to succeeding tax years, subject to a similar limitation.

◆ New Law

The Act increased the maximum allowable deduction for §179 property to $17,500.

Effective Date

This rule applies to property placed in service in tax years beginning after December 31, 1992.

> *Commentary:* The maximum deduction is reduced by the amount by which the cost of §179 property placed in service during the tax year exceeds $200,000. Thus, taxpayers should consider the timing of purchases of §179 property to maximize the tax advantages of the purchases.

WITHHOLDING RATE ON SUPPLEMENTAL WAGES

◆ Prior Law

Supplemental wage payments include bonuses, commissions, and overtime pay that are not paid to an employee concurrently with other wages for the payroll period, or if paid concurrently, are separately stated. Withholding on supplemental wage payments was computed at a rate of 20%, if the employer had elected to do so. Otherwise, the supplemental wages are combined with the regular wages paid for the last preceding payroll period or the current payroll period. The aggregate amount is subject to withholding in accordance with withholding table determinations.

◆ New Law

The elective withholding rate on supplemental wage payments is 28%.

Effective Date

This new rate applies to payments made after December 31, 1993.

EMPOWERMENT ZONES AND ENTERPRISE COMMUNITIES

◆ Prior Law

Some state and local jurisdictions provide enhanced tax benefits and regulatory relief to businesses that locate facilities within designated economically depressed areas, which are usually disadvantaged due to factors such as high crime rates, drug trafficking, lack of economic investment, or high levels of unemployment. The federal government, however, offers no coordinated program that is designed to provide incentives for businesses that locate within such areas.

◆ New Law

The Act provides a number of tax benefits to businesses that locate within economically disadvantaged urban and rural areas that are to be designated in 1994 and 1995 by the Secretaries of Housing and Urban Development (for urban areas) and Agriculture (for rural areas). During that period, nine empowerment zones (six urban and 3 rural) and 95 enterprise communities (65 urban and 30 rural) will be nominated for eligibility to receive the special tax incentives listed below.

Qualifications for Enhanced Tax Benefits

In order to receive the special tax benefits available under the Act for operating a business within an empowerment zone, a business must satisfy specific criteria which are spelled out under the Act, and which undoubtedly will be further clarified in the years ahead by interpretative regulations to be issued by the Internal Revenue Service, Housing and Urban Development (HUD), and the Department of Agriculture. Here is a summary of the *threshold criteria* that must be met. Although these criteria will be subject to refinement upon the issuance of regulations, their general thrust is to ensure that investments are made–and retained–within an empowerment zone in order to spur economic development, and to minimize speculative investments that do not in fact benefit the community to which they are ostensibly meant to apply.

- A qualifying business must actively carry on business within a designated enterprise zone. Limitations are imposed on businesses that are engaged primarily in the leasing of real property or whose sole purpose is holding intangible assets (for example, a franchise agreement) for sale or license. Some types of businesses are expressly excluded from receiving the benefits of locating within an enterprise zone. These include golf courses, massage parlors, hot tub and suntan facilities, racetracks (or other facilities used for gambling), liquor stores, and farms with a value over $500,000.

- Further, a business operating within an enterprise zone must derive at least 80% of its gross income from carrying on business within the zone.

- In regard to its use of property in carrying on its business, the Act generally requires that *substantially all* of the use of tangible property (such as equipment) and intangible property (such as trademarks) occurs within the enterprise zone and is related to the carrying on of the business. No more than 5% of a business's property can consist of such items as financial property, collectibles, and other such items that are normally associated with passive investments as opposed to carrying on an active trade or business.

- Substantially all of the services provided by employees of a business must be performed within the designated zone, and no less than 35% of all employees must be persons who reside within the zone.

Overview of Enhanced Tax Benefits

The Act provides the following special tax benefits to businesses which otherwise meet the eligibility requirements to be an *enterprise zone business*. (Eligibility criteria are discussed above.) These tax benefits are only available during the time which an area is designated an enterprise zone (generally a 10-year period).

Employer Wage Credit. For qualifying businesses, the Act provides a 20% income tax credit (to be phased out beginning in 2002) attributable to employee wages; this credit is subject to a $3,000 cap. The wage credit is only available if the employee to whom it relates actually resides within the enterprise zone and performs substantially all of his or her services related to the enterprise zone business within the designated zone. The credit will be available for both full- and part-time employees. Certain limitations apply to the use of this credit. First, a business must reduce its tax deduction for wages by the amount of the credit claimed each year. Also, a business may not claim the wage credit if it has also utilized the targeted jobs tax credit. (*Note:* If an enterprise zone business is subject to the alternative minimum tax (AMT), the wage credit may offset up to 25% of any AMT liability.)

Equipment Expensing Election. As an alternative to depreciating its cost over many years, the tax code allows smaller businesses to write off a portion of their outlay for equipment expenditures in the year in which the property is placed in service. The Act raised the amount of the cost of such property that may be written off *up front* by all businesses from $10,000 to $17,500. For enterprise zone businesses, however, the Act provides additional benefits. First, an enterprise zone business may annually write off up to $20,000 of the cost of equipment it purchases for use within the enterprise zone. Further, the Act liberalizes the rule that otherwise phases out the benefit of the equipment write-off rule once $200,000 of property is placed in service. For enterprise zone businesses, only one-half of the cost of such equipment is taken into consideration in calculating the $200,000 ceiling.

Tax-Exempt Bonds. The Act creates a new type of

public financing instrument for enterprise zone business—qualified enterprise zone facility bonds. These bonds are intended to help finance the purchase of property by a qualified enterprise zone business. The aggregate face amount of all outstanding enterprise zone bonds for any one enterprise zone business generally may not exceed $3 million. The total outstanding qualified enterprise zone bond financing for each principal user of qualified bonds may not exceed $20 million for all zones and communities.

Effective Date

Empowerment zone and enterprise community designations will be made only during calendar years 1994 and 1995. The tax incentives will be available during the period that the designation remains in effect, which will generally be a period of 10 years.

Commentary: Congress had been evaluating proposals to reinvigorate our cities and other economically depressed areas for some time. Reestablishment of business in economically depressed areas will reduce social cost—by providing an incentive for the creation of jobs in these areas. Although these benefits may not be as generous as some of the original proposals, they will hopefully prove to be a shot in the arm for the much-needed jobs growth in certain sectors of our economy.

Native American Reservation Business Investment Incentives

In addition to the enterprise zone incentives discussed above, the Act also provides tax incentives targeted to spur investment on qualifying Native American reservations (Indian reservations). These incentives are comprised of two components: one tied to investment in property and one tied to the wages and health insurance that an employer pays to a tribal member.

Accelerated Depreciation for Property Investments. The Act allows taxpayers who place in service eligible property (discussed below) on a Native American reservation to claim more rapid depreciation for such property than would otherwise be allowable under the tax code. For example, property which a taxpayer could depreciate over a 3-, 5-, 7-, 10-, 15-, or 20-year life would be reduced to 2-, 3-, 4-, 6-, 9-, and 12-year lives if placed in service on a Native American reservation. Further, nonresidential real property, which under the Act must be depreciated over 39 years, would be eligible for 22-year depreciation. The more rapid recovery periods are allowable even if the taxpayer is subject to the alternative minimum tax.

Qualifying Property. Under the Act, property generally would be eligible for accelerated depreciation if it is used in carrying on business on a Native

American reservation. For this purpose, rental of real property qualifies under the Act, but property used in carrying on gaming activities does not. Also eligible for this benefit is certain property not located on a Native American reservation if its purpose is to connect with property that does qualify for the benefit (e.g., infrastructure such as roads and utility property).

Employer Wage Credit. For qualifying businesses, the Act provides a 20% *incremental* income tax credit attributable to the first $20,000 of qualified wages and employee health insurance costs paid to a tribal member who works on a Native American reservation and lives nearby. *Incremental* means that the employer will only qualify for the credit if the total amount of wages paid increases over time (in order to spur hiring). This benefit is only available if the qualifying employee does not earn more than $30,000 (indexed for inflation after 1994).

Effective Date

The accelerated depreciation benefit applies to property placed in service after December 31, 1993 and before January 1, 2004. The income tax credit for incremental wages applies for wages paid or incurred after 1993, in a tax year that begins before January 1, 2004.

Community Development Corporations (CDCs)

In addition to tax incentives for promoting employment and business investment in Federal empowerment zones, enterprise communities, and on Indian Reservations, the Act includes a new tax incentive for contributions to *community development corporations* (CDCs). Twenty of these entities (at least eight of which must be in rural areas) are to be designated by the Secretary of Housing and Urban Development (HUD) before July 1, 1994.

The Act allows taxpayers to receive an income tax credit for contributions (generally cash or a long-term loan) that they make to a CDC. The contribution must be made to a qualifying CDC (as described above) within five years after the time that the entity is designated as a CDC by HUD. If not in the form of cash, the contribution must be made available for use by the CDC for at least 10 years in its mission of providing employment and business opportunities to individuals who reside within the area to be served by the CDC.

A percentage of the amount of a qualifying contribution to a CDC may be claimed by a taxpayer as a credit. For *cash contributions only,* a contributor may claim a charitable contribution tax deduction in addition to the credit. The credit may be claimed in an amount equal to 5% of the contribution, in annual installments over 10 years. Thus, over the 10-year period a taxpayer would recover 50% of the contribution through the tax credit.

AMORTIZATION OF GOODWILL AND OTHER INTANGIBLE ASSETS

◆ Prior Law

In determining taxable income, a taxpayer is allowed depreciation or amortization deductions for the cost or other basis of intangible property that is used in a trade or business or held for the production of income if the property has a limited useful life which may be determined with reasonable accuracy. However, deductions were not allowed with respect to goodwill or going concern value.

Special rules governed amortization of certain types of intangible assets. For example, acquired computer software generally was amortizable over a five-year period. Lump-sum payments for franchises, trademarks, or trade names were amortized ratably over either 25 years or, if the payment was less than $100,000, over ten years.

Over the years, taxpayers and the IRS have taken different positions on whether certain assets (e.g., customer lists, subscriber lists, patient or client files, insurance expiration lists) that are acquired in connection with the acquisition of an ongoing business are separable from the goodwill of the business. A recent Supreme Court case held that such type of assets can be depreciated if they have useful lives that can be determined with reasonable accuracy.

◆ New Law

The Act allows most acquired intangible assets, including goodwill and going-concern value, to be amortized on a straight-line basis over a uniform 15-year period. The Act also repeals prior-law rules that provided for 10- or 25-year amortization of the cost of franchises, trademarks, or trade names. Thus, certain intangible assets that were not amortizable under prior law are now amortizable over 15 years. Other intangible assets that were amortizable over longer or shorter periods also are subject to 15-year amortization. Generally, no amortization deduction is permitted for self-created intangible assets, i.e., assets created by the taxpayer as opposed to having been obtained through a business acquisition.

In general, the following intangible assets are amortizable over 15 years, on a straight-line basis, if they are *acquired* after August 10, 1993:

- Goodwill;

- Going concern value;

- Workforce in place;

- Information base, including business books and records, operating systems, technical and training manuals, and accounting and inventory control systems;

- Know-how and similar items, including secret formulae, processes, designs, patterns, and similar items. Further, any interest in a film, sound recording, videotape, book, or other similar property that is acquired in connection with the acquisition of a trade or business;

- Customer-based intangibles, including the deposit base of an acquired financial institution, purchased mortgage servicing contracts, investment management contracts, subscription lists, insurance expirations, patient or client files, and advertisers' files;

- Supplier-based intangibles, including favorable supply contracts;

- Government-granted rights, including patents and copyrights acquired in connection with a business acquisition, liquor licenses, FCC licenses, cable TV franchises, taxicab medallions, and airport landing or takeoff rights (or slots);

- Franchises, trademarks, and trade names;

- Covenants not to compete and similar agreements entered into in connection with the direct or indirect acquisition of an interest in a trade or business (or a substantial portion thereof).

Exceptions. The following types of intangible assets are specifically excluded from the 15-year amortization rules:

- Accounts receivable or other similar rights to income for goods and services provided to customers;

- Rights to receive tangible property or services which are not acquired in connection with a business acquisition (such rights would instead be amortized under IRS regulations);

- Interests in a corporation, partnership, trust, or estate;

- Interests in certain financial contracts, including existing futures contracts, foreign currency contracts, notional principal contracts and interest rate swaps;

- Interests in land, including easements, mineral rights, timber rights, grazing rights, riparian rights, air rights, zoning variances, and other similar interests;

- Computer software that is not acquired in connection with the acquisition of a trade or business and computer software (whether or not acquired as part of a business acquisition) that (1) is readily available for purchase by the general public, (2) is subject to a nonexclusive license, and (3) has not been substantially modified (computer software so excluded would be amortized on a straight-line basis over 36 months);

- Interests in films, sound recordings, video tapes, books, or other similar property which are not acquired in connection with a business acquisition;

- Interests in patents or copyrights which are not acquired in connection with a business acquisition;

- Interests under leases of tangible personal property;

- Interests under indebtedness;

- Professional sports franchises;

- The amount of any fees for professional services, and any transaction costs, incurred by parties to a corporate nonrecognition transaction.

Loss Deferral Rule. A loss may not be recognized when a taxpayer disposes of an intangible asset if the taxpayer continues to hold other intangibles that were acquired in the same or a related transaction. Instead, the amount of disallowed loss is allocated to the retained intangibles in proportion to the individual's adjusted basis on the disposition date. Thus, the disallowed loss will be recovered over the remaining term of the original 15-year amortization period that applies to the entire group of retained intangibles.

Commentary: Note that a covenant not to compete (or similar arrangement) that is entered into in connection with an acquisition of assets or stock may not be written off faster than on a straight-line basis over 15 years, even though the covenant expires or otherwise becomes worthless. For example, if a purchaser acquired assets of a trade or business and paid the seller $100,000 per year in each of the five years of the term of the covenant, each payment would have to be capitalized and amortized over the remaining 15-year period, even though the payments are taxable to the covenantor as compensation income in the five years of receipt.

For purposes of these loss deferral rules, members of the same group of controlled corporations and trades or businesses (whether or not incorporated) that are under 50% common control are treated as a single taxpayer.

Commentary: When a taxpayer disposes of an intangible asset at a gain, such gain will be recognized and not deferred. Thus, taxpayers should consider selling intangibles that will produce a loss before selling intangibles that will produce a gain.

EXAMPLE: Three intangibles (Assets A, B, and C) are purchased in the same transaction for $100 each. After the purchase, A increases in value to $150, B declines in value to $50, and C remains worth $100.

1. A sale of A followed by a sale of B results in taxable gain of $50 on A, a disallowed loss of $50 on B, and amortization of C's basis of $150 (i.e., C's original basis increased by the disallowed loss on B) over the remaining period of the 15 years.

2. In contrast, a sale of B followed by a sale of A results in a disallowed loss of $50 on B, allocation of $25 of basis to each of A and C, a $25 gain on the sale of A, and amortization of C's basis of $125 over the remaining period of the 15 years.

Treatment of Nonrecognition Transactions. When an intangible asset is transferred in a nonrecognition transaction or in any transaction between members of the same consolidated group, the transferee *steps into the shoes* of the transferor. Thus, with respect to the amount of its basis in the intangible asset that does not exceed the transferor's basis, the transferee simply continues the transferor's amortization schedule.

Effective Date

Intangible assets acquired after August 10, 1993. In the case of a transfer of an intangible in a nonrecognition transaction, if the transferor would not have been allowed an amortization deduction under the Act with respect to the intangible, then the transferee would not be allowed an amortization deduction except to the extent of the adjusted basis of the transferee that exceeds the adjusted basis of the transferor.

Election for Property Acquired After July 25, 1991. Taxpayers may irrevocably elect to apply the new rules for amortization of intangible assets to all property acquired after July 25, 1991. If a taxpayer makes this election, the Act applies to *all* property acquired after July 25, 1991, both by the taxpayer and by any taxpayer that is under more than 50% common control with the electing taxpayer *at any time* during the period beginning August 2, 1993, and ending on the date that the election is made. It is expected that the IRS will require this election to be made on a timely filed Federal income tax return for the tax year that includes August 10, 1993.

Binding Contract Election. A taxpayer may also elect to apply prior law (rather than the provisions of the Act) to property that is acquired after August 10, 1993 if the property is acquired pursuant to a binding written contract that was in effect on August 10, 1993 and at all times thereafter until the property is acquired.

Anti-Churning Rule. A special rule is designed to prevent taxpayers from converting existing goodwill, going concern value, or any other intangibles for which a depreciation or amortization deduction was not allowable under prior law into amortizable property to which the Act applies. Under this *anti-churning* rule, an intangible that is acquired by the taxpayer after August 10, 1993 is not amortizable if it is goodwill or a going concern value or any other intangible for which a depreciation or amortization deduction would not have been allowable under prior law, if any one of the following conditions is met:

- The intangible was held or used at any time on or after July 25, 1991 and on or before August 10, 1993 by the taxpayer or by a person that is related to the taxpayer or is commonly controlled;

- The intangible was acquired from a person who held such intangible at any time on or after July 25, 1991, and on or before August 10, 1993, and, as part of the transaction, the user of such intangible does not change; or

- The taxpayer grants the right to use the intangible to a person (or a person related to such person) who held or used the intangible at any time on or after July 25, 1991, and on or before August 10, 1993.

The determination of whether the user of property changes as part of a transaction would be made in accordance with IRS regulations.

The anti-churning rule does not apply to an intangible that is acquired from a person with less than a 50% relationship to the acquirer to the extent that: the seller recognizes gain on the transaction with respect to such intangible; and the seller agrees, notwithstanding any other provision of the Code, to pay tax on such gain.

> *Commentary:* The anti-churning rule effectively means that intangible assets that were not amortizable under prior law cannot be amortized under the Act if they are transferred to a related party after August 10, 1993. On the other hand, intangible assets that were eligible for amortization under prior law would have to be amortized over 15-years under the Act if they are transferred to a related party after August 10, 1993.

EXAMPLE: Prior to August 10, 1993, Mr. A conducted Business X as a sole proprietorship. After August 10, 1993, in a tax-free incorporation, Mr. A transfers to Newco all of the assets relating to Business X, including the following intangible assets:

	Full Market Value	*Basis*
Goodwill	100	0
Software	50	20
Workforce	20	0

In consideration for the Business X assets, Mr. A receives 60% of the stock of Newco, plus cash. As a result of receiving *boot*, Mr. A recognizes gain with respect to the intangible assets, and Newco's basis in the intangibles is increased by the respective amounts of such gain.

Because Mr. A is related to Newco, however, the corporation may not amortize any portion of the basis it receives in the goodwill. Likewise, if the workforce is treated as an asset for which no amortization was permitted under current law, Newco may not amortize any portion of the basis it allocates to the workforce.

Pursuant to the special rule for nonrecognition transfers, Newco would step into the shoes of Mr. A with respect to the portion of Newco's basis in the software that does not exceed Mr. A's basis ($20). If the software had two years left in its amortization period in Mr. A's hands, Newco would amortize the $20 over that remaining two-year period. Any increased basis in the software, as a result of the boot given to Mr. A, would be amortized over a 15-year period.

Commentary: For purposes of this anti-churning rule, amounts that were properly amortizable over 25 years pursuant to prior-law are treated as amounts for which depreciation or amortization was allowable under prior law.

Thus, if franchises, trademarks, or trade names are transferred in a taxable transaction to a related party, the transferee may obtain the benefit of an accelerated amortization period, i.e., 15 years compared to the 25-year period used by the transferor.

REPEAL OF STOCK-FOR-DEBT EXCEPTION

◆ Prior Law

Generally, if a debt owed by a taxpayer is discharged without the taxpayer having to give money or property in satisfaction of the debt, the amount of the debt discharged must be included in the gross income of the taxpayer. The amount included in income is often referred to as cancellation of indebtedness (or *COD*) income. Taxpayers are allowed to exclude COD income from gross income if it occurs when the taxpayer is insolvent or in a title 11 case (bankruptcy); however, such taxpayers must reduce certain tax attributes by the amount of the excluded COD income. An insolvent taxpayer may not exclude COD income in excess of the amount by which the taxpayer is insolvent.

The amount of COD income generally is the difference between the adjusted issue price of the debt being canceled and the amount of cash and the value of any property used to satisfy the debt. Thus, if a debtor corporation transfers its stock to a creditor in satisfaction of a debt, the corporation realizes COD income equal to the excess of the adjusted issue price of the debt over the fair market value of the stock transferred.

Under the judicially created stock-for-debt exception (as modified by the Internal Revenue Code), a corporation that issued stock to its creditors did not recognize COD income, or reduce its tax attributes, if the corporation was in a title 11 bankruptcy case or to the extent that the corporation was insolvent. The stock-for-debt exception did not apply if the taxpayer issued certain types of preferred stock, token shares of stock, or if the stock was transferred on a relatively disproportionate basis to unsecured creditors.

◆ New Law

The Act repeals the stock-for-debt exception. Consequently, in all cases, a corporate debtor's use of stock to extinguish a debt will be treated in the same manner as the use of any other corporate property, and the corporation will be treated as having satisfied the debt with an amount of money equal to the fair market value of the stock transferred. Thus, the corporation will realize COD income to the extent the adjusted issue price of the debt exceeds the value of the stock. If the corporation is in a Title 11 bankruptcy case or is insolvent, the corporation will not have COD income, but will reduce certain tax attributes.

Effective Date

Generally, the stock-for-debt exception will not apply to any stock transferred after December 31, 1994, in satisfaction of any debt. A transitional rule provides that the Act does not apply to any transfer of stock in satisfaction of debt in a title 11 bankruptcy case that was filed on or before December 31, 1993.

> *Commentary:* The Act eliminates the tax advantage to bankrupt or insolvent companies of issuing stock, as opposed to cash or other property, to creditors in partial satisfaction of debt. Furthermore, without the opportunity to avoid reducing their tax attributes, some companies that might have reorganized under prior law may now be forced into liquidation. The December 31, 1993 bankruptcy filing transitional rule could cause a flood of filings by the close of this year.

EXPANSION OF TAX ATTRIBUTES REDUCED BY CANCELLATION OF INDEBTEDNESS

◆ Prior Law

Generally, if a debt owed by a taxpayer is discharged without the taxpayer having to give money or property in satisfaction of the debt, the amount of the debt discharged must be included in the gross income of the taxpayer. The amount included in income is often referred to as cancellation of indebtedness (or *COD*) income. A taxpayer may exclude COD income from gross income if it occurs in a title 11 bankruptcy case or when the taxpayer is insolvent (to the extent of the insolvency); however, the taxpayer's tax attributes must be reduced by the amount of the excluded COD income.

The following tax attributes were reduced, in the following order, by the amount of any COD income excluded from gross income:

1. Any net operating loss for or carryovers to the tax year of discharge;

2. Any carryovers to or from the tax year of the discharge used in determining the general business credit;

3. Any net capital loss for or carryovers to the tax year of discharge;

4. The basis of the property of the taxpayer; and

5. Any carryovers to or from the tax year of discharge used in determining the foreign tax credit of the taxpayer.

The passive activity loss and credit rules limit the amount of deductions and credits generated by a passive activity which a taxpayer may use for the tax year. Deductions from passive activities generally may only be used to offset income from passive activities, and may not be deducted against active income, such as wages. Similar rules apply to tax credits from passive activities. Passive activity deductions and credits that are not used in a tax year are carried over and may be used in subsequent tax years. Any unused deductions and credits may be used in full when the taxpayer disposes of the interest in the passive activity to an unrelated person. Passive activity losses and credits were not tax attributes that were subject to reduction by excluded COD income.

If a taxpayer pays alternative minimum tax (AMT), the amount of the AMT paid generally is allowed as a credit against the taxpayer's regular tax in subsequent years. The minimum tax credit carried forward to a subsequent tax year cannot be used to reduce tax below the tentative minimum tax in the subsequent year. The AMT credit was not a tax attribute that was subject to reduction by excluded COD income.

◆ New Law

The Act adds the AMT credit and passive activity losses and credits to the list of tax attributes that are reduced in the case of discharge of indebtedness that is excludable from income. Therefore, the list of tax attributes, in the order in which they are reduced, is as follows:

1. Any net operating loss for or carryovers to the tax year of discharge;

2. Any carryovers to or from the tax year of the discharge used in determining the general business credit;

3. Any minimum tax credit available as of the beginning of the tax year following the tax year of discharge;

4. Any net capital losses for or carryovers to the tax year of discharge;

5. The basis of the property of the taxpayer;

6. Any passive activity loss or credit carryover from the tax year of discharge; and

7. Any carryovers to or from the tax year of discharge used in determining the foreign tax credit of the taxpayer.

The amount of reduction is generally one dollar for each dollar of excluded COD income, except that in the case of credits the reduction is 33-1/3 cents for each dollar of excluded income.

Effective Date

This rule is effective for COD income that is excluded in tax years beginning after December 31, 1993.

> *Commentary:* If the amount of COD excluded from income is greater than the total attributes available for reduction, the taxpayer is not required to recognize the excess as income for tax purposes. The addition of the passive activity loss and credit carryovers and minimum tax credits to the list of attributes required to be

reduced will diminish the possibility of this benefit.

STATE AND LOCAL BUSINESS TAX CONSIDERATIONS

While most businesses (and individuals) have been worrying about how much their federal taxes will rise, you should consider that you may be paying more in state income taxes as well. That's because most states tax corporations by reference to federal taxable income or federal income tax liability. So provisions that affect your federal taxable income could have a rollover effect on your state and local income taxes.

The effect of the federal changes will vary from state to state. For one thing, states may adopt different effective dates for the federal changes. Some states' laws base state tax liability on federal law as of the date the return is filed, but laws in other states will require legislative action to incorporate these federal changes into the state law. Many state legislatures are out of session right now and therefore cannot act immediately to adopt the federal provisions. This may result in a transition period when state tax liabilities are required to be computed under a state law that differs from the federal law. And in many instances, states will not adopt retroactive reinstatement of lapsed federal provisions as the federal government has done. For example, federal tax law, and accordingly most state tax laws, provided an income exclusion for educational expenses that were reimbursed by an employer (see the discussion on page 110). The federal exclusion expired July 1, 1992. Although Congress reinstated the exclusion retroactively as of July 1, 1992, for federal purposes, that does not guarantee that state legislatures will reinstate the exclusion retroactively for state income tax purposes. When computing state taxable income, taxpayers may have to add back income that is excluded under federal law.

The ultimate effect of the Act on state tax liabilities is still up in the air, as state legislatures may be expected to consider new legislation to modify the effect of the federal legislation on their budgets. Because the United States is a federalist form of government, federal and state governments share authority and responsibilities. During the past decade, the federal government has attempted to deal with a growing budget imbalance by shifting responsibility of many social programs to the states through reductions in federal funding. Although this may have resulted in a short-term benefit to the federal budget, budget crunches were felt at the state and local levels of government. Unlike the federal government, most states must maintain balanced budgets. Thus efforts to reduce the federal deficit have forced most state and local governments to increase revenues in order to provide the same benefits and protections.

From a policy perspective, the Act may suggest that Congress and the Administration have developed a stronger sense of the need for greater cooperation among all levels of government to resolve the nation's social and economic problems. This is supported by the fact that the Act raises federal revenues in ways that will have the least effect on state and local tax (SALT) systems. First, tax increases tend to focus on income tax rate increases rather than base broadening. Second, the legislation avoids revenue sources traditionally relied upon by state and local governments, such as excise and consumption taxes. And spending provisions addressing programs such as Head Start and child immunization programs may relieve states of some of the funding burden for popular social programs. But although the legislation attempts to deal with the federal budget deficit in a way that does not merely shift funding responsibilities to state and local budgets, it is not likely that states can avoid all the effects of federal budget tightening.

Credits and Other Proposals With No Flow-Through Effect. A number of items that are significant for federal purposes may have little or no effect on state taxes. States generally provide for separate tax credits that are unrelated to the federal tax credits. Therefore, the research and development credit and the targeted jobs tax credit generally will not affect a corporation's state income tax burdens.

SALT Relief. For corporate income taxes, only a few states allow a deduction for federal income taxes. Although the new provisions could mean an automatic tax decrease in these states, some states may consider higher tax rates to compensate for the tax base loss.

Enterprise Zones. The federal enterprise zones provision should cause taxpayers to focus on state enterprise zone incentives. States have used incentives for many years to attract or retain businesses, but the opportunities are often overlooked when a business plans to move or expand its existing operations. If you are planning expansion, you should consult a specialist for assistance in securing tax incentive opportunities.

Although the Act further restricts deferral of federal income tax on certain foreign affiliates' earnings, the income that is recognized for federal purposes may not be taxable under state and local tax laws. Many states currently provide a dividends-received deduction for dividends received from U.S. affiliates. Under the U.S. Supreme Court's ruling in *Kraft v. Iowa*, the Foreign Commerce Clause requires these states to provide a dividends-received deduction for dividends received from foreign affiliates as well. Therefore, income that is recognized as a dividend under these federal provisions may qualify for the state dividends-received deduction.

3

◆ ◆ ◆ ◆ ◆ ◆ ◆

COMPENSATION AND BENEFITS CHANGES

EMPLOYER-PROVIDED EDUCATIONAL ASSISTANCE

◆ Prior Law

Generally, job-related education provided by or paid for by employers is excludable from an employee's gross income as a working condition fringe benefit. In addition, education provided by or paid for by employers under an *educational assistance program* is excludable from an employee's gross income, regardless of whether the education is job-related. In order to qualify for this latter exclusion, amounts have to be paid under a program that satisfies specific requirements, e.g., it is provided on a nondiscriminatory basis, has an annual dollar limit of $5,250 per employee, and provides written documentation and employee notice. The exclusion for amounts paid or incurred under employer-provided educational assistance programs expired on June 30, 1992.

◆ New Law

Under the Act, the exclusion for employer-provided educational assistance programs is retroactively extended through December 31, 1994. In addition, the Act makes clear that any employer-paid or employer-provided education not provided under an *educational assistance program* is excludable if the education is sufficiently job-related to qualify as a working condition fringe.

Effective Date

The extension is effective retroactive to July 1, 1992; all amounts paid or incurred on or after that date for qualified educational assistance are excludable from income. The clarification relating to educational assistance provided as a working condition fringe is effective retroactively for all tax years beginning after December 31, 1988.

Commentary: The conference agreement did not adopt the House proposal that provided specific relief provisions for recoupment of excess taxes paid with respect to educational assistance provided after June 30, 1992 and for employers and employees who excluded educational assistance expenses on the assumption that the statutory exclusion would be retroactively extended. However, the Conference Report indicates the conferees' intent that Treasury use its existing authority to alleviate administrative problems that may result from the expiration and retroactive reinstatement of the exclusion and to facilitate in the simplest way possible the recoupment of excess taxes paid with respect to educational assistance provided in the last half of 1992.

EXTENSION OF TARGETED JOBS TAX CREDIT

◆ Prior Law

Employers are entitled to receive a tax credit for hiring individuals from several targeted groups, including the economically disadvantaged, the disabled, or the recipients of payments under certain public assistance programs. The credit generally equals a maximum of 40% of $6,000 of the wages paid to most target group members in their first year of employment and 40% of $3,000 of first year wages paid to certain economically disadvantaged student summer workers.

The credit expired with respect to employees who began work after June 30, 1992.

◆ New Law

The targeted jobs tax credit is extended for any amount paid or incurred to an individual who begins work on or before December 31, 1994.

Effective Date

The extension is retroactively effective with respect to employees who began work with the employer after June 30, 1992.

> *Commentary:* Employers who hired individuals belonging to any of the targeted groups after June 30, 1992, and who have filed their 1992 tax returns should file amended 1992 returns in order to obtain the credit. Employers who have calculated any 1993 estimated tax payments without considering the credit should adjust any remaining 1993 estimated tax payments to take the credit into account.

REDUCED COMPENSATION FOR QUALIFIED RETIREMENT PLAN PURPOSES

◆ Prior Law

For purposes of determining a participant's benefit under a tax-qualified retirement plan, no more than $200,000 in annual compensation, indexed annually for inflation, can be taken into account. The limit for 1993 is $235,840. This limit also applies for purposes of determining the amount of an employer's deductible contribution to the plan.

The limit is intended to result in increased proportionate benefits to lower-paid employees. By treating them as if they receive less compensation for purposes of calculating contributions or benefits, those employees with actual compensation above the limit are considered, for plan purposes, to be receiving greater benefits as a percentage of pay. The employer is then required, in order to satisfy the nondiscrimination rules, to provide that same percentage to non-highly compensated employees.

◆ New Law

The Act further limits the benefits which can be provided to highly compensated employees by reducing the amount of compensation which can be taken into account for qualified retirement plan purposes. The new limit is $150,000, indexed annually for inflation (in increments of $10,000) beginning in 1995.

Changes in the Qualified Plan Compensation Limit

1988 — No Limit	1992 — $228,860
1989 — $200,000	1993 — $235,840
1990 — $209,200	1994 — $150,000
1991 — $222,220	

Effective Date

The new limit generally applies to benefits accruing in plan years beginning after December 31, 1993. Previously accrued benefits are grandfathered and special transition rules are provided for certain governmental plans.

Commentary 1: There are two broad categories of employees that will be directly affected by the $150,000 cap on compensation. First, those employees who are earning more than $235,840 could lose over 35% of their future benefits in their employer's qualified plans, e.g., in the case of a 10% profit sharing plan, the contributions allocated to someone earning $235,840 or more will drop from $23,584 to $15,000. The second category of adversely affected employees consists of individuals earning between $150,000 and $235,840. These individuals will have their benefits reduced by an amount which varies according to their compensation in excess of $150,000.

Commentary 2: Employers have three broad alternatives with respect to the new $150,000 cap. First, they can do nothing and simply provide lesser benefits to their highly paid employees. Second, they could make these employees whole by increasing benefits within their qualified plan. This would mean, for some employers, an increased cost of maintaining their qualified plan of more than 35%. While this cost can be reduced through various changes in the plan's design (e.g., instituting permitted disparity), such changes will tend to be an expensive way of making the executives whole since they will usually involve increasing benefits for a broad-based group of employees earning less than $150,000. Third, the employer can provide additional benefits for those employees earning in excess of $150,000 through a nonqualified retirement arrangement. While these arrangements would allow the employer to target specific employees, they have the disadvantage of either resulting in current income to the covered employees or leaving their benefit subject to the claims of the employer's creditors. Finally, employers, particularly those with 401(k) plans, should review their administrative and record keeping procedures to ensure that benefits and contributions will be calculated under the new limit beginning with the 1994 plan year in order to avoid having to refund or recalculate contributions during the year.

EXECUTIVE COMPENSATION—DEDUCTION LIMITATIONS

◆ Prior Law

The gross income of an employee includes any compensation received for services rendered. An employer was allowed a corresponding deduction for reasonable salaries and other compensation. Whether compensation is reasonable is determined on a case-by-case basis. However, the reasonableness standard has been used primarily to limit payments by closely held companies where nondeductible dividends may be disguised as deductible compensation. The reasonableness standard rarely affected publicly held companies.

◆ New Law

A publicly held corporation will not be allowed a deduction for compensation paid or accrued with respect to a *covered employee* to the extent such compensation exceeds $1 million for the tax year. A corporation's covered employees for a tax year are the chief executive officer of the corporation (or an individual acting in such capacity) and the four highest compensated officers (other than the chief executive officer) whose compensation is required to be disclosed to shareholders under Securities and Exchange Commission (SEC) rules. If SEC disclosure is required with respect to fewer than four executives (other than the chief executive officer), then only those executives are covered employees. If an individual is a covered employee for a tax year, then the $1 million limitation applies to all compensation not explicitly excluded from the limitation, regardless of whether the compensation is for services as a covered employee and regardless of when the compensation was earned.

Compensation explicitly excluded from the $1 million cap includes:

- Compensation payable on a commission basis;

- Certain other performance-based compensation;

- Payments to a tax-qualified retirement plan (including salary reduction contributions);

- Amounts excludable from the executive's gross income, such as employer-provided health benefits and certain other fringe benefits, and;

- Any compensation payable under a written binding contract which was in effect on February 17, 1993 and all times thereafter before such compensation was paid and which was not modified thereafter in any material respect before such compensation was paid.

Performance-based compensation (other than commissions) is exempt from the $1 million cap only if (1) it is paid solely on account of the attainment of one or more performance goals, (2) the performance goals are established by a compensation committee consisting solely of two or more outside directors, (3) the material terms under which the compensation is to be paid, including the performance goals, are disclosed to and approved by the shareholders in a separate vote prior to payment, and (4) prior to payment, the compensation committee certifies that the performance goals and any other material terms were in fact satisfied.

In order to be performance-based, compensation must be paid pursuant to a pre-established objective formula or standard that precludes discretion. This generally means that a third party with knowledge of the relevant performance results could calculate the amount to be paid. The *Conference Committee Report* indicates Congress's intent that what constitutes a performance goal be broadly defined and include, for example, a goal that is applied to the individual executive, a business unit, or the entire corporation. Stock options that are granted with an exercise price at least equal to the stock's fair market value on the date of grant will be treated as performance-based provided that the outside director and shareholder approval requirements are met; there is no need to certify that the performance standards have been met.

Effective Date

These rules apply to compensation that is otherwise deductible by the corporation in a tax year beginning on or after January 1, 1994 unless, as described above, such compensation is payable under a binding written contract which was in effect on February 17, 1993.

Commentary 1: Faced with the $1 million cap on deductible compensation, publicly held corporations are almost certain to restructure their compensation packages for covered employees to ensure that as much compensation as possible is performance-based. In addition, incentive stock options, which do not in any event generate a deduction for employers (where certain holding period requirements are met) may become increasingly attractive for employers that are running up against the $1 million cap for covered employees.

Commentary 2: In the case of performance-based compensation paid pursuant to a plan other than a stock option plan, the shareholder approval requirement generally is satisfied if the shareholders approve the specific terms of the plan, including the class of executives to which it applies. For a stock option plan, the shareholders generally must approve the specific terms of the plan, the class of executives to which it applies, the option price (or formula under which the price is determined), and the maximum number of shares subject to the option that can be awarded to any executive under the plan. It appears that *specific* executives do not have to be approved.

4

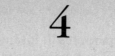

PROVISIONS AFFECTING THE FINANCIAL SERVICES INDUSTRY AND INVESTMENT INTERESTS

MARK TO MARKET FOR SECURITIES DEALERS' INVENTORIES

◆ Prior Law

Dealers in securities were required for Federal income tax purposes to maintain inventory based on one of three methods: (1) cost, (2) lower of cost or market value, or (3) market value, the so-called *mark to market* method. If the cost method were used, unrealized gains and losses with respect to the securities were not taken into account for Federal income tax purposes. If inventories were valued at lower of cost or market, a method in which the inventory is valued at market value only if that amount is below cost, unrealized losses (but not unrealized gains) with respect to the securities were taken into account for Federal income tax purposes. Under the mark to market method, which requires valuing the inventory at fair market value at year end, both unrealized gains and losses with respect to the securities were taken into account for Federal income tax purposes.

◆ New Law

The Act requires a dealer in securities to mark to market all the securities which it holds at year end, both securities it holds as inventory and all other securities it holds, except for securities which the dealer has properly identified as being held for investment or otherwise not subject to the mark to market rules.

The term *security* is broadly defined by the provisions. It includes (1) stock in a corporation; (2) partnership or beneficial ownership interests in a widely held or publicly traded partnership or trust; (3) any note, bond, debenture or other evidence of indebtedness; (4) any interest rate, currency or equity notional principal contract; (5) any evidence of an interest in, or a derivative financial instrument in any security described above, or any currency, including options, forward contracts, short positions or similar financial instrument in such a security or currency, except for certain contracts traded on a regulated securities market which are already required to be marked to market; and (6) any position which is not itself a security described above, but which is a hedge with respect to any security described above, and which is clearly identified as such in the dealer's records before the close of the day on which it was acquired or entered into.

The new mark to market rules apply only to dealers of securities. However, if a taxpayer meets the definition of a dealer, the rules will apply to all types of securities held by that taxpayer whether or not the taxpayer regards himself as a dealer with regard to that type of security. A dealer is defined as one who *regularly purchases from and sells securities to customers in the ordinary course of a trade or business*, or *regularly offers to enter into, assume, offset, assign or otherwise terminate positions in securities with customers in the ordinary course of a trade or business.*

As noted above, the mark to market provisions apply to all securities, whether held as inventory or otherwise. Under the rules, a security held as inventory by a dealer is required to be included in inventory at its fair market value. Similarly, any other security held by the dealer at the close of a tax year and not subject to one of the exceptions to the mark to market rules must be treated as sold for its fair market value on the last business day of the tax year.

There are certain exceptions to the mark to market rules. They do not apply to a security held for investment, or to a security which is a hedge with respect to (1) a security to which new Internal Revenue Code section 475(a) does not apply, or (2) a position, right to income, or a liability which is not a security in the hands of the taxpayer. To the extent provided in regulations, the exception will not apply to certain notional principal contracts and derivative financial instruments held by a dealer in such interests. Furthermore, these exceptions will not apply unless the dealer identifies the security as a valid exception before the close of day on which the security was acquired or entered into. In addition, a special rule for banks and thrifts states that loans and other evidences of indebtedness will not be subject to the mark to market provisions if they are not held for sale. It is unclear how this exception differs from the general exception for securities held for investment.

The *Conference Committee Report* indicates that financial institutions which originate and sell loans in the ordinary course of business may have additional time to identify loans as held for investment. The report states that regulations should allow financial institutions that originate and purchase loans in the ordinary course of their business to identify loans as held for investment (i.e., not held for sale) based on their accounting practices. Regulations should allow financial institutions up to 30 days to make the identification.

The *Conference Committee Report* also directs that regulations be issued minimizing the accounting burdens that the identification rules will have on a taxpayer's hedge accounting. It cites, as an example, the problems created in trying to determine which portion of a "global hedge" should be marked to market. Regulations should allow for reliance on the taxpayer's internal accounting systems to make that determination.

The penalties for improper identification are severe. If a taxpayer improperly identifies a security as excepted from the mark to market rules or fails to identify a hedge of a security as subject to the mark to market rules, then the mark to market rules will apply to such a security or position. In addition, any loss realized by reason of the application of the mark to market rules to such an improperly identified security or position is to be recognized only to the extent of gain previously recognized under the rules. Any loss so disallowed will be recognized upon disposition of the security or position.

If a security is properly excepted from mark to market accounting under the rules described above, and the security subsequently fails to qualify for this exception, the mark to market rules will apply to future changes in the value of the security relative to its value at the time such failure occurs. Any gain or loss attributable to the period during which the security was not subject to the mark to market rules will be deferred until the security is sold. However, once a security becomes subject to the mark to market rules, it continues to be subject to such rules even if the dealer subsequently holds the security for investment purposes only.

Generally, any gain or loss taken into account under the mark to market rules is treated as ordinary gain or loss. However, the ordinary characterization does not apply to any gain or loss allocable to any period during which the security (1) is a hedge of an item which is not a security within the mark to market definition, (2) is held by the taxpayer in a capacity other than as a dealer, or (3) is improperly identified by the taxpayer.

The inventory capitalization rules are not applicable to securities subject to the mark to market rules.

The Act contains a grant of regulatory authority for the issuance of regulations as necessary or appropriate to carry out the purposes of the mark to market rules, including rules to prevent the avoidance of mark to market through the use of year-end transfers, related parties, or other arrangements. In addition, regulations may apply the rules to any security which is a hedge which cannot be identified with a specific security, position, right to income, or liability.

EXAMPLE: An investment bank, in its ordinary course of business, regularly purchases and sells stock and bonds (*securities*) to the public. Under this provision, the investment bank would be treated as a dealer in securities and subject to these rules even though some of its securities' purchases are held for investment. The investment bank would have to identify those securities it intends to hold for investment on the day they are acquired. Since the investment bank separately identifies its investment portfolio, these securities would not be subject to the mark to market rules. The *inventory* securities and all other securities that are not identified as held for investment would be subject to this provision.

Effective Date

The mark to market rules apply to all tax years ending on or after December 31, 1993. Taxpayers are permitted to treat the application of the rules as a change in accounting method. The net adjustment resulting from the accounting method change is to be taken into income ratably over a five-year period beginning with the first tax year ending on or after December 31, 1993. Certain floor specialists and market makers using the LIFO inventory method may take the amount of the net adjustment attributable to the use of LIFO into account ratably over a 15-year period. The *Senate Finance Committee Report* states that taxpayers will have 30 days after the date of enactment to identify securities which are held on the date of enactment as qualifying for one of the exceptions to the mark to market rules.

Commentary: Two problems will confront taxpayers as they attempt to comply with the mark to market rules: (1) classification and identification, and (2) valuation. Due to the effective date of the provision, taxpayers will need to address the classification issue immediately and assess their systems to ensure that they are capable of identifying securities not subject to the rules.

The rule makes an attempt at resolving the *Arkansas Best* issue in which business-related losses are often treated as capital, while the gains are treated as ordinary. It achieves a partial resolution to this problem by requiring that any gain or loss appropriately taken into account under the mark to market rules is treated as ordinary. However, the *Arkansas Best* problem remains for many transactions outside these rules.

The term *dealer* is very broad and not clearly defined in the statute or the legislative history. It is unclear what level of activity will cause a financial institution to be treated as a dealer. For example, when does the occasional securitization of automobile loans or the participation of loans rise to a sufficient level of activity to cause the institution to be classified as a dealer for the mark to market provisions? It is unlikely that a definitive answer to this question will be known until regulations are issued.

FEDERAL ASSISTANCE PAYMENTS MADE TO CERTAIN THRIFTS

◆ Prior Law

Prior to the passage of the Financial Institutions Reform, Recovery, and Enforcement Act of 1989 (FIRREA), federal financial assistance received by a troubled thrift institution from the Federal Savings and Loan Insurance Corporation (FSLIC) was tax-exempt. Some of this assistance was in the form of compensation for the difference between the book value and sales proceeds of *covered assets*. Covered assets are assets classified as nonperforming or troubled at the time of the assisted transaction. Furthermore, the basis of assets was not reduced for the amounts of FSLIC assistance received. Thus, institutions were able to claim a loss on the disposition or charge-off of the covered asset at the same time that they were being reimbursed for all or a portion of the loss by the FSLIC. However, another section of the Code provides that a taxpayer can claim a deduction for a loss on the sale or other disposition of property to the extent that the taxpayer's adjusted basis for the property exceeds the amount realized on the disposition and the loss is not compensated, for example, by insurance. In 1991, a Treasury Report recommended that the FSLIC assistance received on covered assets should be treated as compensation similar to insurance for purposes of determining the loss or bad debt deduction associated with such assets.

◆ **New Law**

Any FSLIC assistance received upon the disposition of an asset is to be taken into account as compensation in determining the amount of any loss on disposition of the asset. Similarly, any FSLIC assistance with respect to a debt is to be taken into account for purposes of determining whether the debt is worthless (or the extent to which the debt is worthless) and in determining the amount of any addition to a reserve for bad debts arising from the worthlessness or partial worthlessness of the debt.

When a taxpayer disposes of an asset, the Act allows no deduction for any loss incurred to the extent the assistance agreement contemplates a right to receive FSLIC assistance for the loss. Additionally, a thrift institution is not permitted to charge the loss against the bad debt reserve and is not permitted a deduction for any amount reimbursed by the FSLIC. FSLIC assistance taken into account under this provision will not be treated as a net positive adjustment in determining adjusted current earnings for AMT.

Effective Date

The provision applies to FSLIC assistance credited on or after March 4, 1991, for (1) assets disposed of and charge-offs made in tax years ending on or after March 4, 1991, and (2) assets disposed of and charge-offs made in tax years ending before March 4, 1991, but only for the purpose of determining the amount of net operating loss (NOL) carryover in a tax year ending on or after March 4, 1991. Financial assistance is considered credited when a taxpayer makes an approved debit entry to the Special Reserve Account required to be maintained under the assistance agreement to reflect the asset disposition or write-down.

> *Commentary:* No inference is intended as to prior law or as to the treatment of any item to which this provision does not apply. The Treasury Department has announced its intention to seek, through litigation, to apply the same rule contained herein to FSLIC assistance credited prior to the effective date.

LIMITATION ON USE OF CAPITAL GAIN GENERATORS AND OTHER CONVERSION TECHNIQUES

Because there now exists a substantial differential between the tax rates on ordinary income and those on capital gains, Congress deemed it necessary to curtail certain techniques which could be used by taxpayers to generate capital gains without a significant risk of loss. This curtailment affects five areas: capital gain conversion transactions, extension of the market discount rules, stripped preferred stock, the definition of investment income, and substantially appreciated inventory held by a partnership.

Capital Gain Conversion Transactions

◆ Prior Law

Under prior law, taxpayers were able to generate capital gains without a significant risk of loss by means of certain transactions which were economically similar to loans, but which, because of their form, permitted taxpayers to treat the return from the transaction as capital in nature.

◆New Law

The Act provides that a portion of capital gain arising from certain designated *conversion transactions* will be recharacterized as ordinary income. Transactions will be designated as *conversion transactions* if substantially all of the taxpayer's expected return from a transaction is attributable to the time value of the taxpayer's net investment in the transaction and the transaction meets one of the following four criteria. The four criteria are: (1) the acquisition of property accompanied by a substantially contemporaneous contract to sell such property, or substantially identical property, at a predetermined price, (2) certain straddles, (3) any transaction which is marketed or sold as producing capital gains, or (4) any transaction specified as a conversion transaction in regulations.

The amount of gain to be recharacterized will not exceed the amount of interest that would have been earned on the taxpayer's net investment in the property at a rate equal to 120% of the applicable Federal rate for the period of time that the taxpayer held the investment. This limit may be reduced to reflect prior recognition of ordinary income items from the conversion transaction and in other appropriate circumstances. Although the gain will be recharacterized as ordinary, it will not be recharacterized as interest.

A special rule exempts options dealers and commodities traders from the provisions, but anti-abuse rules prevent limited partners or entrepreneurs from unduly profiting by this exception.

Effective Date

The provision applies to all conversion transactions entered into after April 30, 1993.

Commentary: The provision to curtail what Congress views as the abusive conversion of ordinary income into capital gain is intended to be broad. However, many issues in the provision to eliminate capital gain conversion transactions remain open to interpretation. Until regulations are issued, brokers and taxpayers will no doubt continue their attempts to devise instruments and tailor transactions which obtain favorable tax treatment. Taxpayers purchasing financial instruments or entering into transactions which could potentially be construed as conversion transactions should consult their tax advisers.

Extension of the Market Discount Rules

◆ Prior Law

Market discount can be broadly defined as the difference between the face amount of a debt instrument and the price paid for that debt instrument, exclusive of original issue discount. The market discount rules require that market discount on a bond be accrued over time, and that upon disposition of a market discount bond any gain be treated as ordinary income to the extent of accrued market discount. However, under a grandfathering rule, taxpayers acquiring tax-exempt obligations and bonds issued prior to July 18, 1984, could treat any market discount on those bonds as capital gain rather than as ordinary income.

◆ New Law

The Act extends the market discount rules to market discount bonds issued on or before July 18,

1984. The Act also extends the rules requiring that gain on the sale or other disposition of a market discount bond be treated as ordinary income to tax-exempt obligations. Thus, gain on the disposition of such bonds will be treated as ordinary income to the extent of accrued market discount.

Effective Date

This provision is effective for bonds purchased after April 30, 1993. Thus, holders of these bonds who acquired their bonds prior to May 1, 1993, will not be affected by this provision.

Treatment of Purchaser of Stripped Preferred Stock

◆ Prior Law

Under prior law, if redeemable preferred stock was stripped of its dividend rights, the stripped stock was not subject to the stripped bond rules which treat the stripped instruments as original issue discount instruments and require inclusion of a portion of the original issue discount (OID) in income annually.

◆ New Law

Stripped preferred stock is treated as if it were a bond issued on the purchase date having original issue discount equal to the excess of the redemption price of the stock over the purchase price of the stock. The purchaser of stripped preferred stock is treated as though he had acquired a stripped bond with OID and must include such OID in income in accordance with the OID rules. The person who strips preferred stock and disposes of the dividend rights is treated as though he had purchased the stripped preferred stock on the date of the disposition for a purchase price equal to his adjusted basis in such stripped preferred stock and he is subject to the OID rules on such stock.

The provision applies to preferred stock that is limited and preferred as to dividends, does not participate to any significant extent in corporate growth, and that has a fixed redemption price.

Effective Date

The provisions are effective for purchases of stripped stock or dispositions of dividend rights on stripped stock on or after April 30, 1993.

Commentary: Due to tax uncertainty, the use of stripped preferred stock was rarely, if ever, implemented.

Elimination of Capital Gain From Definition of Investment Income

◆ Prior Law

For taxpayers other than corporations, the deduction for interest on indebtedness allocable to investment property is limited to net investment income for the year. Net investment income was defined as the excess of investment income over investment expenses. The definition of investment income included gross income from property held for investment and any net gain (either ordinary or capital) attributable to the disposition of property held for investment.

◆ New Law

The Act intends to prevent taxpayers from taking a deduction at the top marginal rate for ordinary income while the net investment income for the year includes income taxed at a preferential capital gains rate. Under the Act, net capital gain attributable to the disposition of property held for investment is no longer includable in the definition of investment income for purposes of computing the investment interest deduction limitation. However, a taxpayer may elect to include net capital gain amounts in investment income for this purpose if the taxpayer also agrees to reduce his net capital gain eligible for the 28% maximum capital gains rate by the same amount.

Effective Date

This provision is effective for tax years beginning after December 31, 1992.

Treatment of Substantially Appreciated Inventory Held by a Partnership

◆ Prior Law

Amounts received by partners in exchange for partnership interests were treated as ordinary income to the extent of substantially appreciated inventory. Also, exchanges between a partnership and a partner of substantially appreciated inventory for interests in other partnership property or vice versa are treated as taxable sales or exchanges rather than as nontaxable distributions. For this purpose, the definition of substantially appreciated inventory is inventory whose value exceeds both 120% of its adjusted basis and 10% of the value of all partnership property (other than money).

◆ New Law

The Act eliminates the 10% value of partnership property requirement. Thus, inventory of a partnership will be considered to be substantially appreciated if its fair market value exceeds 120% of its adjusted basis to the partnership. For purposes of this calculation, any inventory property acquired in order to avoid the substantially appreciated designation by increasing the base on which the 120% is calculated is disregarded.

Effective Date

This provision is effective for sales, exchanges, and distributions after April 30, 1993.

5

◆ ◆ ◆ ◆ ◆ ◆ ◆

PROVISIONS AFFECTING REAL ESTATE

The following specific new law provisions affect real estate: affordable housing incentives (low-income rental housing credits and mortgage revenue bonds), passive activity loss liberalization, pension fund investment in real estate, elective deferral of phantom income from debt workouts, and lengthened recovery periods for commercial property. Also, a provision dealing with partnership redemptions is covered that applies to partnerships operating in most industries, including real estate. In addition to these specific provisions impacting the real estate industry, it is important to emphasize that a significant tax rate differential has opened up between ordinary income and capital gains. Real estate held for investment or used in a trade or business produces capital gains except to the extent of depreciation recapture. Thus, the favorable capital gains rate differential produced by the new law will generally benefit the real estate industry and perhaps induce some investment in real estate where market factors otherwise justify the investment.

LOW-INCOME RENTAL HOUSING TAX CREDIT

◆ Prior Law

Owners of newly constructed or substantially rehabilitated low-income housing units are entitled to a tax credit in annual installments over 10 years. The credit generally provides the owner with a tax credit equal to the present value of 70% of the *qualified basis* of low-income housing units. A tax credit equal to the present value of 30% of the *qualified basis* is available in other cases. To qualify for the credit, the owner must receive a low-income housing credit allocation from the appropriate state credit authority. The low-income rental housing tax credit expired June 30, 1992.

◆ New Law

The low-income housing credit is reinstated retroactively to July 1, 1992 and made permanent. In addition, changes have been made to several technical provisions (as to which other effective dates may apply), including the addition of a *de minimis* exception for violations of the tenant-occupancy requirements.

Commentary 1: The low-income housing credit is extremely popular in Congress and in the real estate industry. National housing policy has come to rely on the public/private partnerships that have used the low-income housing credit to expand the nation's stock of affordable housing. Low-income housing credits are popular with large corporations because the credits reduce the effective corporate tax rate. Further, because the credit continues for ten years, an investment produces a stream of predictable benefits for the corporation. An ancillary benefit is received because the corporate investor is seen as providing an important social benefit by helping to house the homeless. For banks, the investment may also satisfy community reinvestment goals or regulatory requirements.

Commentary 2: Uncertainty as to the availability of the credit has somewhat inhibited the market for low-income housing credit deals in the past. Now that the credit is permanent, the creation of low-income housing through public/private partnerships should increase.

MORTGAGE REVENUE BONDS

◆ Prior Law

State and local jurisdictions can issue tax-exempt qualified mortgage bonds (*QMBs*) to finance the purchase or improvement of owner-occupied residences within certain targeted areas. QMBs effectively provided borrowers with an interest rate subsidy. Persons receiving QMB-backed loans must be first-time home-buyers and satisfy a home purchase price, borrower income and other requirements. In addition, the governmental unit can elect to reduce its authority to issue QMBs and instead issue mortgage credit certificates (*MCCs*). MCCs entitle home-buyers to a nonrefundable income tax credit of a specified percentage of the mortgage interest paid each year.

◆ New Law

The authority to issue QMBs and MCCs is reinstated *retroactively* to July 1, 1992, and made permanent.

PASSIVE ACTIVITY LOSS LIBERALIZATION

◆ Prior Law

The passive activity rules limit deductions and credits from passive trade or business activities. Deductions attributable to passive activities, to the extent they exceed income from passive activities, generally may not be deducted against other income, such as wages, portfolio income, or business income that is not derived from a passive activity. Deductions that are suspended under these rules are carried forward and are treated as deductions from passive activities in succeeding years. Suspended losses are allowed in full when a taxpayer disposes of his or her entire interest in a passive activity to an unrelated person.

Generally, a trade or business activity is passive unless the taxpayer *materially participates* in that activity. Rental real estate activities, however, are passive regardless of the level of the taxpayer's participation. A special rule permits the deduction of up to $25,000 of losses from certain rental real estate activities (even though they are considered passive) if the taxpayer actively participates in them. This special rule is available in full to taxpayers with AGI of $100,000 or less and phases out for taxpayers with AGI between $100,000 and $150,000.

◆ New Law

The Act liberalizes the passive activity limitations for certain real estate professionals. Taxpayers who satisfy certain eligibility thresholds and materially participate in rental real estate activities may offset these rental real estate losses against all sources of taxable income.

Commentary 1: The Act permits qualifying real estate professionals to carry back or forward a net operating loss from rental real estate activities to offset *any* kind of income. However, suspended losses from any rental real property activity that is treated as not passive by reason of the new law are treated as losses from a former passive activity. Thus, such suspended losses are limited to income from the activity, and are not allowed to offset other income. When the taxpayer disposes of his entire interest in the activity in a fully taxable transaction with an unrelated party, any remaining suspended losses allocable to the activity are allowed in full.

Commentary 2: Individuals may want to consider deferring from 1993 to 1994 certain cash basis deductions relating to material participation rental real estate activities, thereby avoiding treatment as former passive activity deductions in favor of treatment as nonpassive deductions in 1994.

Eligibility. Only individuals and closely held C corporations can qualify for this special rule. An individual taxpayer will qualify for any tax year if more than one-half of the personal services (with more than 750 hours) performed in trades or businesses by the taxpayer during such a tax year are performed in real property trades or businesses in which the taxpayer materially participates. Personal services performed as an employee are not considered in determining material participation unless the employee has more than a 5% ownership in the employer. However, independent contractor realtor services would qualify for this purpose. For closely held C corporations, the eligibility requirements are met if more than 50% of the corporation's gross receipts for the tax year are derived from real property trades or businesses in which the corporation materially participates.

EXAMPLE: During 1994, a self-employed real estate developer earned $100,000 in development fees from projects the developer spent 1,200 hours developing. In addition, the developer incurred rental real estate losses of $200,000 from properties which the developer spent over 800 hours managing during 1994. The developer performs no other personal services during the year, and has no other items of income or deduction. Since the developer (1) materially participated in the rental real estate activity, (2) performed more than 750 hours in real property trades or businesses, and (3) performed more than 50% of the developer's total personal service hours in real estate trades or businesses in which the developer materially participated, the developer will have a net operating loss of $100,000 to carry back (and the excess to carry forward) to offset any source of income.

Commentary: This passive loss relief is a two step process. First, taxpayers must demonstrate eligibility for the relief provision through achieving the required levels of personal services in real estate trades or businesses. Thereafter, eligible taxpayers get relief from the passive loss limitations only for their rental real estate activities for which they satisfy the material participation standards.

For spouses filing joint returns, each spouse's personal services are taken into account separately. However, in determining material participation, the participation of the other spouse is taken into account as required under current law.

Commentary: A husband and wife filing a joint return meet the eligibility requirements if, during the tax year, *one spouse* performs more than 750 hours representing at least half of his or her personal services in a real estate trade or business in which either spouse materially participates.

Real Property Trade or Businesses. A real property trade or business includes any real property development, redevelopment, construction, reconstruction, acquisition, conversion, rental, operation, management, leasing, or brokerage trade or business.

Scope of Rental Real Estate Activities. Whether a taxpayer *materially participates* in his or her rental real estate activities is determined generally as if each interest of the taxpayer in rental real estate is a separate activity. However, the taxpayer may elect to treat all interests in rental real estate as one activity.

Commentary: The election permitting a taxpayer to aggregate his or her rental real estate activities for testing for material participation is not intended to alter present law with respect to material participation through limited partnership interests. Generally, no interest as a limited partner is treated as an interest with respect to which a taxpayer materially participates. However, Treasury regulations provide that a limited partner is considered to materially participate in the activities conducted through the partnership in certain situations where 1) the limited partner is also a general partner at all times during the partnership's tax year, 2) the limited partner participates in the partnership activity for more than 500 hours during the tax year, 3) the limited partner materially participates in the activity during any five of the preceding ten years, or 4) the activity is a personal service activity in which the limited partner materially participated for any three preceding years.

Other. Losses allowed under the present-law $25,000 allowance are determined before the application of this provision.

Effective Date

Tax years beginning *after* December 31, 1993.

PENSION FUND AND OTHER INVESTMENTS IN REAL ESTATE

◆ Prior Law

In general, a qualified pension trust or an organization that is otherwise exempt from income tax is taxed on unrelated business taxable income (UBTI). Certain types of income, including rents, royalties, dividends, interest, and gains or losses on the disposition of non-dealer property are excluded from UBTI, except when such income is derived from debt-financed property. Income from debt-financed property is generally treated as UBTI in proportion to the amount of debt financing. An exception to the debt-financed property rules is available to pension trusts, educational institutions, and certain other exempt organizations (*qualified organizations*) that make debt-financed investments in real property, but only if certain technical requirements are met.

An exempt organization's share of income from a publicly traded partnership automatically was treated as UBTI regardless of the source of the income. Dividends paid by a real estate investment trust (REIT) were not UBTI, unless the stock in the REIT was debt-financed. For purposes of testing for REIT qualification, a domestic pension trust was treated as a single individual when determining whether more than 50%, in value of, REIT outstanding stock was owned, directly or indirectly, by five or fewer individuals (*the five or fewer rule*).

◆ New Law

Debt Financed Real Property: Restrictions on debt-financed real estate investments by qualified organizations are relaxed through (1) liberalization of the sale-leaseback prohibition, (2) permission of certain seller financing, and (3) relaxation of fixed sales price and participating loan restrictions for certain real property acquired from financial institutions.

Effective Date

Acquisitions (and leases entered into) on or after January 1, 1994.

Investments in Publicly Traded Partnerships: The rule automatically treating income from publicly traded partnerships as UBTI is repealed. The determination of whether income from a publicly traded partnership is UBTI is made as if the income had been realized directly by the partner.

Effective Date

Partnership tax years beginning on or after January 1, 1994.

Dealer Rule: Gains and losses from the disposition of real property and mortgages that a qualified organization acquired from a financial institution that is in conservatorship or receivership (*disposal* *property*) are excluded from the *dealer rule*, and not treated as UBTI. This exception applies to properties designated as disposal property within nine months of acquisition, and disposed of within two-and-a-half years of acquisition. No more than one-half, by value, of properties acquired in a single transaction may be designated as disposal property. Property will not qualify for the exception if improvements to the property exceed 20% of the selling price of the property.

Effective Date

Property acquired on or after January 1, 1994.

Investments in REITs: The rules for determining whether there is sufficient diversity of ownership to qualify for REIT status are relaxed with respect to investment by domestic pension trusts by adopting a *look-through* approach to determine whether the five or fewer rule is met. Beneficiaries of a domestic pension trust will now be treated as holding stock in the REIT in proportion to their actuarial interests in the trust, thus placing domestic and foreign pension investment in REITs on a level playing field. However, certain pension trusts owning more than 10% of the REIT must treat a percentage of dividends from the REIT as UBTI if the REIT itself has UBTI and it qualified as a REIT by reason of this legislative modification of the five or fewer rule. Such UBTI treatment for a percentage of REIT dividends applies only if (1) one pension trust owns more than 25% of the value of the REIT or (2) a group of pension trusts individually holding more than 10% of the value of the REIT collectively own more than 50% of the REIT.

Effective Date

Tax years beginning on or after January 1, 1994.

Other: Premiums from unexercised options on real property, and from the forfeiture of good-faith deposits for the purchase, sale, or lease of real property, and loan commitment fees will not be treated as UBTI. Title-holding companies will be permitted to receive UBTI (that would otherwise disqualify tax-exempt status of the company) up to 10% of its gross income for the tax year, if the UBTI is incidentally derived from the holding of real property.

Effective Date

Premium or fees received on or after January 1, 1994; title-holding company tax years beginning on or after January 1, 1994.

Commentary: These new law provisions are targeted to pension fund investment in real estate and real estate securities — REIT stocks. From a policy standpoint, the provisions are designed to make it easier for pension funds and certain other tax exempt organizations to become more significant players in the real estate markets, thereby expanding the pool of capital available for real estate investment and financing. With REITs having become the real estate investment vehicle of choice for the 1990s, it is possible that pension funds could provide substantial capital through REITs. However, in recent years pension funds have learned some painful lessons about real estate valuation cycles. Also, for those pension funds desiring to make additional real estate investments, the advantage of market liquidity arising from making the investment through REIT stocks is weighed against advantages to the pension fund of controlling the real estate through direct ownership of the property.

DISCHARGE OF REAL PROPERTY BUSINESS INDEBTEDNESS

◆ Prior Law

The discharge of indebtedness generally gives rise to gross income to a debtor taxpayer. However, discharge of indebtedness income is excluded from income if it occurs in a bankruptcy case when the taxpayer is insolvent, or arises from certain farm indebtedness. The amount currently excluded from income under these exceptions is applied to reduce tax attributes (e.g., net operating loss carryovers, basis in property, etc.) of the taxpayer. Certain reductions of purchase money debt between an original purchaser and original seller are treated as purchase price adjustments, so that the purchaser reduces basis in acquired property in lieu of recognizing income. Prior to its repeal by the Tax Reform Act of 1986, an election was available to solvent taxpayers permitting them to reduce basis in assets in lieu of recognizing debt discharge income arising from certain qualified business indebtedness.

◆ New Law

The Act provides an election for solvent taxpayers (other than C corporations) to exclude from income the discharge of qualified real property business indebtedness. The amount excluded cannot exceed the basis of depreciable real property of the taxpayer and is treated as a reduction in such basis. The basis reduction is treated as depreciation for purposes of computing any ordinary income recapture on a subsequent disposition of the property.

Qualified Real Property Business Indebtedness. This is defined as secured indebtedness incurred or assumed prior to January 1, 1993, in connection with real property used in a trade or business. Indebtedness incurred or assumed on or after January 1, 1993, qualifies if (1) it is incurred to refinance qualifying pre-January 1, 1993, debt (but only to the extent of debt being refinanced), or (2) it is incurred to acquire, construct, or substantially improve real property that is secured by such debt.

Limitations. The amount of debt discharge income that can be excluded is subject to two limitations, a fair market value limitation and an overall basis limitation. The excluded amount may not exceed the excess of the principal amount of the debt (immediately before the discharge) over the fair market value (immediately before the discharge) of the real property which is security for the debt. For this purpose, the fair market value of the property is reduced by the outstanding principal amount of any other qualified real property business indebtedness secured by the property.

EXAMPLE: Assume on July 1, 1993, Individual J owns a building worth $150,000, used in his trade or business, that is subject to a first mortgage debt of $110,000 and a second mortgage debt of $90,000. J agrees with his second mortgagee to reduce the second mortgage debt to $30,000, resulting in discharge of indebtedness income in the amount of $60,000. Assuming that J has sufficient basis in business real property to absorb the reduction, J can elect to exclude $50,000 of that discharge from gross income. The $50,000 amount is the excess of $200,000 combined mortgage debts over the $150,000 fair market value of the real estate immediately before the discharge. The excess $10,000 of debt relief in this example is currently taxable because the taxpayer's wealth is currently enhanced by the creation of $10,000 net fair market value equity in the property.

An overall limitation also applies so that the currently excluded amount of debt discharge income cannot exceed the aggregate adjusted bases (determined as of the first day of the next tax year or, if earlier, the date of disposition) of depreciable real property held by the taxpayer immediately before the discharge (excluding any property acquired in contemplation of such discharge).

Basis Reduction. The amount of excluded income is applied to reduce the basis of business real property held by the taxpayer at the beginning of the tax year following the tax year in which the discharge occurs. If the taxpayer disposes of real property prior to the first day of the next tax year, then the reduction in basis of such property is made as of the time immediately before the disposition.

Depreciation Recapture. If depreciable real property, the basis of which was reduced under this provision, is disposed of, then for purposes of determining the amount of depreciation recapture: (1) any such basis reduction is treated as a deduction allowed for depreciation, and (2) the determination of what would have been the depreciation adjustment under the straight-line method is made as if there had been no such reduction. Thus, the amount of the basis reduction that is recaptured as ordinary income is reduced over the time the taxpayer continues to hold the property, as the taxpayer forgoes depreciation deductions due to the basis reduction.

Partnerships. If debt discharge occurs in a partnership, the partnership determines whether the discharge qualifies for the exception. The election to apply the provision, however, is made by each partner. A partner's interest in a partnership is treated for basis reduction purposes as depreciable real property to the extent of the partner's proportionate interest in the depreciable real property held by the partnership. The partnership's basis in depreciable real property, with respect to an electing partner, is correspondingly reduced to the extent the partner reduces basis in his or her partnership interest.

S Corporations. S corporations make the election to apply the provision, and the income exclusion and basis reduction are both made at the S corporation level.

Effective Date

Debt discharges after December 31, 1992 in tax years ending after that date.

Commentary: This elective basis reduction provision is a response to the great volume of debt discharge income being generated from workouts of real estate in our current economy.

Prior to 1986, this type of relief was available to all businesses. The new law restores the relief to the real estate industry at a time when real estate values are depressed and property owners are faced with phantom income from debt workouts that produce no cash with which to pay the resulting tax liability. Because the elective relief from current income exclusion must be accompanied by a decrease in the basis of depreciable real property, the relief constitutes a tax deferral rather than a tax forgiveness. With respect to properties whose bases have been adjusted, future depreciation deductions are lowered and larger gains are realized on disposition.

PARTNERSHIP REDEMPTIONS

◆ Prior Law

The tax treatment of a payment made in liquidation of the interest of a retiring or deceased partner in a partnership is determined by whether the payment is made in exchange for the partner's interest in partnership property. A liquidation payment made in exchange for such property is treated as a distribution by the partnership. The partner receiving the distribution will only recognize gain from the distribution to the extent the cash distributed exceeds the partner's adjusted basis in the partnership interest.

At the partnership level, a payment made in liquidation that is not made in exchange for the partner's interest in partnership property may be treated in one of two ways for tax purposes. If the amount of the payment is determined without reference to partnership income, it is treated as a guaranteed payment and is generally a deductible expense of the partnership. If the amount of the payment is determined by reference to partnership income, the payment is treated as a distributive share of partnership income to the retiring partner, thereby reducing the distributive shares of other partners, which is equivalent to a deductible expense of the partnership.

Under prior law, payments made in liquidation of the interest of a partner attributable to goodwill (except to the extent the partnership agreement provided for such payments) or unrealized receivables of the partnership were not treated as payments in exchange for an interest in partnership property. (Generally, unrealized receivables were defined for purposes of this rule as unbilled amounts, accounts receivable, and a number of other items, such as depreciation recapture.) Thus, such payments were effectively deductible expenses of the partnership upon redemption of a partner. Congress was concerned that this rule allowed the partnership a current deduction for an expenditure that is normally considered capital in nature.

◆ New Law

In certain cases, the Act repealed the special rule for payments made in liquidation of the interest of a partner in goodwill or unrealized receivables. Thus, such amounts are treated as payments for the partner's interest in partnership property, which would not give rise to a deductible expense by the partnership or a decrease in the other partners' distributive shares of partnership income.

If the retiring or deceased partner is a general partner and capital is not a material income producing factor in the partnership, payments to the partner for goodwill or unrealized receivables will continue to be treated as payments not in exchange for an interest in partnership property. Where substantially all the income of the partnership relates to personal services performed by the partnership, capital is not a material income producing factor. Also, payments made to a retiring partner as compensation for past services performed by the partner will continue to be deductible.

Commentary: For all limited partners in all partnerships and general partners in partnerships in which capital is a material income-producing factor (e.g., real estate assets), payments for goodwill and unrealized receivables will not be deductible by the partnership. Partnerships which hold significant real estate assets *and* conduct fee-based businesses may want to segregate their fee-earning operations into separate partnerships so that capital is not a material income-producing factor for the services partnership and any payments to retiring or deceased general partners for goodwill associated with the fee-producing activities remain deductible.

The Act also repealed the special rule for payments for unrealized receivables, other than unbilled amounts and accounts receivable, regardless of whether capital is a material income-producing factor of the partnership. Thus, for example, a payment relating to depreciation recapture would be treated as made in exchange for the interest of the retiring or deceased partner's interest in partnership property.

Effective Date

Generally, the new law applies to partnership redemptions on or after January 5, 1993. However, the new law will not apply to such redemptions if a binding, written contract that specifies the amount and timing of payments was in effect on January 4, 1993, and at all times thereafter.

DEPRECIATION OF NONRESIDENTIAL REAL PROPERTY

◆ Prior Law

For regular tax purposes, the amount of the depreciation deduction allowed with respect to nonresidential real property for any tax year was determined by using the straight-line method and a recovery period of 31.5 years. For AMT purposes, a recovery period of 40 years was used.

◆ New Law

For regular tax purposes, depreciation for nonresidential real property is determined by using a recovery period of 39 years. For AMT purposes, the recovery period of 40 years is retained.

Effective Date

Generally, property placed in service on or after May 13, 1993. Transition rules generally prevent the new longer recovery period from applying to property placed in service before January 1, 1994, if before May 13, 1993, either construction commenced or a binding written contract to purchase or construct the property existed.

Commentary: As applicable to leasehold improvements, the lengthened recovery period further distorts the allocation of depreciation deductions over the term of a lease. This is particularly harsh to small businesses or companies that lease significant amounts of real estate, such as retailers. In order to reduce the impact of this provision, lessees may likely want to structure leases to require the lessor to make the real property improvements and recover their cost through increased rents over the term of the lease. This allows lessees current rent deductions over the term of their lease equal to the economic cost of the leasehold improvements, rather than smaller depreciation deductions during the lease term followed by a write-off of the remaining cost basis upon lease termination. This strategy highlights the tension between lessors and lessees caused by the rules applicable to leasehold improvements. In cases where a lessor owns the tenant improvements, the lessor will receive increased rents during the lease term, but it is the position of the IRS that recovery of the capital expenditure for leasehold improvements must continue for the duration of the 39-year recovery period even though the tenant's lease has expired.

The distortion of income caused by these provisions has caught the attention of some members of Congress. An exception to the statutory recovery period for leasehold improvements to more closely match the lease term has been suggested for future legislation.

6

◆ ◆ ◆ ◆ ◆ ◆ ◆

PROVISIONS AFFECTING MULTINATIONAL CORPORATIONS

TRANSFER PRICING COMPLIANCE

◆ Prior Law

A penalty is imposed in the amount of 20% of tax on under-payments attributable to certain transfer pricing allocations that constitute substantial valuation misstatements. For this purpose, a substantial valuation misstatement arises if (1) the transfer price for any property or services (or for the use of property) claimed on a return is 200% or more (or 50% or less) of the amount determined to be the arm's-length price, or (2) the net transfer price adjustment exceeds $10 million. The penalty is increased to 40% in the case of gross valuation misstatement, i.e., if (1) the transfer price for any property or service claimed on a return is 400% or more (or 25% or less) of the amount determined to be the arm's-length price, or (2) the net transfer price adjustment exceeds $20 million.

Transfer pricing adjustments are excluded for purposes of the penalty if there was *reasonable cause* for the taxpayer's determination of the transfer price and the taxpayer acted in good faith. The requirements to satisfy this exclusion are not set forth in the statute, but are prescribed in proposed regulations. Under those regulations, a taxpayer may be excepted from penalty if the transfer price reported on the return is supported by a transfer pricing study, contemporaneously documented when the return is filed, and if the taxpayer reasonably believes that the result of the transfer price would more likely than not be sustained on its merits (*more-likely-than-not standard*).

◆ New Law

The new law extends the reach of the penalties by lowering the dollar amount threshold as follows:

- The substantial understatement (20% penalty) threshold amount of $10 million under existing law is changed to the lesser of $5 million or 10% of gross receipts.

- The gross understatement (40% penalty) threshold amount of $20 million under existing law is changed to the lesser of $20 million or 20% of gross receipts.

The new law also liberalizes the conditions precedent to the good faith and reasonable cause exception to penalties. The more-likely-than-not standard of the proposed regulations is abandoned. Instead, taxpayers must show that the transfer pricing method used was reasonably applied in a manner consistent with the regulations. Such determination must be contemporaneously documented at the time the return is filed and provided to the IRS within 30 days of request. Taxpayers using *unspecified methods* (so-called *other methods*) have the additional burden of showing that (1) none of the specified methods were likely to result in a price that would clearly reflect income, and (2) the unspecified method would likely result in a price that would clearly reflect income.

Effective Date

Tax years beginning after December 31, 1993.

Commentary: The new law is supplemented with a transfer pricing enforcement initiative. The IRS has not attempted to apply the transfer pricing penalty since the provision was enacted in 1990, in part, because no definition of the reasonable cause and good faith exclusion had been provided by statute. By statutorily defining this exclusion, Congress intends that the IRS will have sufficient guidance to apply the penalty. Given the substantial penalty that could be imposed, taxpayers will be more likely to establish and document transfer pricing methods contemporaneously.

Commentary: With the new enhanced transfer pricing penalties, taxpayers may want to take the following steps:

- **Consider an Advance Pricing Agreement with the IRS.** The new law provides little certainty as to what constitutes a transfer pricing method reasonably applied. Although a taxpayer may document the reasonableness of a particular method, the IRS may, with hindsight, disagree. An Advance Pricing Agreement (APA) is a binding agreement between the taxpayer and the IRS which provides certainty as to the correct transfer pricing method used during the period covered by the agreement.

- **Perform a transfer pricing study and document the results.** The best means of avoiding the penalties, outside of an APA, is to conduct a transfer pricing study. The study should support the transfer pricing method being used and the results as reported on the tax return. The study should be contemporaneously documented.

- **Develop and document a transfer pricing policy.** The policy should provide guidance to company personnel as to how to set transfer prices and select transfer pricing methods that are consistent with the arm's-length standard. Since a policy must have a sound theoretical basis consistent with the regulations, this alternative may be best combined with one of the previous alternatives. The more evidence available which indicates that management has set transfer prices with an eye toward the arm's-length standard, the better the chance of avoiding the transfer pricing penalty.

- **Document and justify current transfer pricing method.** Companies should contemporaneously document the transfer pricing method used and provide a discussion of why the company believes the method is reasonable. However, there is no guarantee that this alternative will satisfy the reasonable cause and good faith exception. It is not a substitute for a proper transfer pricing study. Nevertheless, it may indicate a good faith effort.

ALLOCATION OF R&E EXPENSES

◆ Prior Law

United States taxpayers may claim a foreign tax credit for foreign income taxes paid. The foreign tax credit is limited to the United States tax liability on foreign source taxable income. To compute this limitation, deductions for expenses must be allocated to gross income from domestic and foreign sources. Allocation of an expense to foreign source gross income reduces foreign source taxable income and thus reduces the amount of foreign tax credit that a taxpayer may claim.

A Treasury regulation issued in 1977 provides generally that the research and experimentation (R&E) expense may be allocated to domestic and foreign source gross income based on either the taxpayer's relative amounts of domestic and foreign source gross income in the appropriate product category or the taxpayer's relative gross sales receipts from domestic and foreign sources in the product category. If the sales method is chosen, the taxpayer may first allocate 30% of its R&E expense to sales from the location where most of its R&E activity is conducted (usually the United States, in the case of a United States taxpayer).

Treasury regulations regarding the allocation of R&E, introduced in 1977, have been modified eight times by temporary legislation. Each temporary legislative rule permitted direct allocation of a substantial percentage (ranging from 50% to 100%) of the expense associated with United States-based R&E to domestic source income, whether or not the expense actually related to such income. The most recent statutory rule permitted taxpayers to allocate 64% of United States-based R&E expense to domestic source income. This statutory rule expired in mid-1992, but an IRS announcement (Rev. Proc. 92-56) permits taxpayers to continue to apply the 64% rule for an additional 18-month period.

◆ New Law

The new law will permit taxpayers to allocate 50% of United States-based R&E expense to domestic source income and 50% of foreign-based R&E expense to foreign source income. The remaining R&E will be allocated on the basis of gross income or sales.

Effective Date

This provision will apply for only one year: the tax year (beginning on or before 8/1/94) that commences immediately following the taxpayer's last tax year to which Rev. Proc. 92-56 applies, or would have applied had the taxpayer elected to use the Revenue Procedure.

DEFERRAL OF TAX ON FOREIGN EARNINGS AND CHANGES TO THE PASSIVE FOREIGN INVESTMENT COMPANY REGIME

◆ Prior Law

Generally, the Code does not tax income earned by a foreign corporation until the earnings are repatriated to United States shareholders. The Code provides exceptions to this general deferral rule by requiring the recognition of foreign earnings whether or not they are repatriated. These rules which accelerate recognition are called the Subpart F rules and the passive foreign investment company (PFIC) rules.

Under the Subpart F rules, a 10% United States shareholder of a controlled foreign corporation (CFC) is required to include in income currently its pro rata share of the *Subpart F income* of the CFC.

Under the PFIC rules, a United States shareholder of a PFIC is subject to provisions designed to eliminate the benefit of deferral of United States tax on the shareholder's pro rata share of the PFIC's total undistributed earnings. These provisions apply regardless of the United States shareholder's percentage ownership. A PFIC is any foreign corporation (whether or not a CFC) if (1) 75% or more of its gross income for the tax year is passive income, or (2) 50% of its assets (determined on a FMV basis) produce, or are held for the production of, passive income. For this purpose, passive income generally does not include active banking or insurance income. A United States shareholder of a PFIC may elect to include currently in income its pro rata share of the PFIC's total earnings. If this election is not made in a timely manner, the United States shareholder is subject to an interest charge when it receives certain distributions from the PFIC or disposes of the PFIC stock.

The PFIC regime contains look-through rules, whereby a corporation that owns 25% or more of the value of the stock of another corporation is treated as owning that proportionate part of the other corporation's assets and income. Moreover, interest, dividends, rents and royalties received from certain related parties that are not subject to the general look-through treatment explained above are excepted from treatment as passive income to the extent that those amounts are allocable to income of the payor that is not passive income. The characterization of the assets that generate the income will follow the characterization of the income the asset generates. Thus, for example, a loan to a related person will be treated as a passive asset only if the interest on the loan is treated as passive income.

Under current law, United States shareholders of CFCs may defer United States tax on the CFC's earnings that are not Subpart F income, unless the earnings are repatriated or the PFIC rules apply. Many United States shareholders are able to defer U.S. tax on active foreign earnings indefinitely by deferring dividends and managing their passive income and assets so as to avoid the PFIC thresholds.

◆ New Law

Inclusions based on excess passive assets. The new law would require 10% United States shareholders of certain CFCs to include in income currently their pro rata share of a specified portion of the CFC's current and accumulated earnings. The provision would generally apply to a CFC holding passive assets representing 25% or more of the total assets of the CFC. The portion of current and accumulated earnings subject to inclusion (*includible earnings*) would be the lesser of (1) total current and accumulated earnings and profits accumulated in tax years beginning after September 30, 1993, or (2) the amount of excess passive assets.

The amount of excess passive assets would equal the amount by which the average amount of passive assets held by a CFC as of the close of each quarter exceeds 25% of the average of the CFC's total assets held at the close of each quarter. For this purpose, passive assets would be defined as under the PFIC rules (including the definition of passive income thereunder). Includible earnings would be adjusted to account for earnings previously taxed.

For CFCs, or other electing foreign corporations, passive assets would be valued at adjusted tax basis rather than fair market value. However, solely for purposes of this new rule and for purposes of determining whether a CFC is a PFIC, CFCs would be allowed to compute a deemed tax basis for intangibles equal to R&E expenses for the current year plus the two preceding years, plus 300% of royalty payments made during the tax year to unrelated persons and related U.S. persons. Payments made to related foreign persons are not taken into account.

CFCs in a *CFC group* will be tested together as a single corporation to determine excess passive assets. If a CFC group has excess passive assets, the aggregate excess passive asset amount will be allocated among the CFCs in the CFC group on the basis of each CFC's relative earnings. A CFC group means one or more chains of CFCs connected through stock ownership of a top-tier CFC if:

- The top-tier CFC owns directly more than 50% (by vote or value) of the stock of at least one of the other CFCs; and

- More than 50% (by vote or value) of the stock of each of the CFCs (other than the top-tier) is owned directly or indirectly by one or more other members of the group.

Additional PFIC Changes. Certain leased property will be treated as assets held by a foreign corporation for purposes of the PFIC asset test. The rule will apply to tangible personal property with respect to which the foreign corporation is the lessee under a lease with a term of at least 12 months.

A securities broker or dealer exclusion from PFIC status is provided similar to the active banking and insurance exclusion. The new excess passive asset provision (§956A) is coordinated with PFICs by providing that inclusions of income by U.S. shareholders due to the investment of earnings in U.S. property, or ownership of excess passive assets, will be treated as distributions for purposes of computing the interest charge on excess distributions to U.S. shareholders of PFICs that are controlled foreign corporations.

Effective Date

Tax years beginning after September 30, 1993.

> *Commentary:* Taxpayers who are shareholders of CFCs will now be required to manage the amount of passive assets even more closely than under the PFIC regime. Planning in this area will largely involve making decisions to repatriate the amount of excess passive assets or invest in other foreign active businesses. Moreover, taxpayers may wish to reorganize foreign ownership structures in order to take advantage of the CFC grouping rules.

> The new law closes the existing *§956 deemed distribution loophole* in the existing PFIC rules. Therefore, taxpayers need to consider whether an affirmative §956 inclusion during 1993 would eliminate the possibility of an excess distribution from a PFIC in coming years.

OTHER MODIFICATIONS TO SUBPART F/SAME COUNTRY EXCEPTION

◆ Prior Law

U.S. shareholders are taxed currently on their proportionate share of a controlled foreign corporation's passive type income (foreign personal holding company income). While interest and dividends are normally Subpart F income, certain dividends and interest received from a related corporation organized and operated in the same foreign country are excluded from the Subpart F definition.

◆ New Law

The same country exception to Subpart F income in the case of certain dividends received from related controlled foreign corporations will be limited as follows: dividends will not qualify for the same country exception to the extent that the distributed earnings and profits were accumulated by the distributing corporation during periods prior to the CFC shareholder holding the stock, either directly or indirectly. The legislative history for this provision indicates that the legislation intends that no inference be drawn as to the proper interpretation of prior law.

Effective Date

Tax years beginning after September 30, 1993.

MODIFICATION TO THE INVESTMENT OF EARNINGS IN U.S. PROPERTY RULE

◆ Prior Law

U.S. shareholders of controlled foreign corporations are required to include in income their pro rata share of the foreign corporation's earnings invested in U.S. property.

◆ New Law

The new law revises the rules for earnings invested by a controlled foreign corporation in U.S. property so that they parallel those that govern the treatment of excess passive assets, described above. The new rules require:

- The determination of the investment in U.S. property on a quarterly basis.

- Actual distributions during the year and their impact on the determination of available unrepatriated earnings and profits will be considered before determining the inclusion (e.g., actual distributions now have priority).

- The §956 inclusion amount will be determined as the lesser of two amounts:

  —U.S. property, less earnings previously taxed under §956, or

—The CFC's current and accumulated earnings and profits, less accumulated earnings previously included under either §956 or §956A.

- The §956 income inclusion determined above would be reduced by previously taxed Subpart F earnings.

A special adjustment to the amount of the investment in U.S. property applies where U.S. property was acquired before the foreign corporation became a CFC. In this case, the amount of U.S. property held by the CFC will not include specific items of U.S. property owned by a foreign corporation prior to becoming a CFC to the extent of the earnings of the foreign corporation which were accumulated prior to becoming a CFC.

Effective Date

Tax years beginning after September 30, 1993.

POSSESSION TAX CREDIT

◆ Prior Law

Domestic corporations with business operations in United States possessions may elect a credit to eliminate the United States tax on certain income related to their possession-based operations. The credit spares the electing corporation from United

States tax whether or not it pays income tax to the possession. The possessions tax applies to business income from the possession and income from certain investments (qualified possession source investment income, or QPSII).

In order to qualify for the possession tax credit, a domestic corporation must derive at least 75% of its gross income from the active conduct of a trade or business within a possession over a three-year period, and at least 80% of the corporation's gross income must be derived from sources within a possession during that period.

◆ New Law

The possession tax credit remains available to businesses operating in U.S. possessions; however, the credit for business income would be limited by subjecting it to one of two alternative limitations, the *percentage limitation* or the *economic activity limitation*. In order to use the percentage limitation, the taxpayer must elect to do so for the first tax year beginning after 1993 for which it claims a possession credit. All affiliated corporations must use the same method. The determination of the credit for QPSII is unchanged.

The percentage limitation would be the possession credit, as computed under prior law, multiplied by 60% for the first year, 55% the second year, 50% the third year, 45% the fourth year, and 40% the fifth year and all years thereafter.

The second possible limitation (*economic activity limitation*) would be a credit equal to the sum of (1) 60% of qualified compensation, (2) a portion of the depreciation deduction for property located within the possession and used in the active conduct of the possession corporation's trade or business, and (3) if the corporation has not elected the profit-split method for allocating income from intangible property, a portion of the possession income tax it incurred during the tax year. Regarding (2) above, the portion allowed will be the indicated percentage of the current year's depreciation deduction:

- Short-life (3- or 5-year) tangible property: 15%

- Medium-life (7- or 10-year) tangible property: 40%

- Long-life (all other) tangible property: 65%

For purposes of the limitation, qualified compensation is the sum of (1) qualified possession wages (eligible wages are limited to 85% of the maximum earnings subject to social security withholding (currently 85% of $57,600 or $48,960)), and (2) employee fringe benefit expenses. Wages are defined with reference to the Federal Unemployment Tax Act (FUTA) definition. An affiliated group may elect to consolidate and treat all related possessions corporations as one corporation for purposes of determining its possession credit under the economic activity limitation.

Effective Date

Tax years beginning after December 31, 1993.

Commentary 1: Taxpayers will need to decide whether to use the percentage limitation as the appropriate limitation in determining their possession credit. To use the percentage limitation, a corporation must elect to use that limitation for its first tax year for which it claims the possession credit after 1993.

Commentary 2: Because the economic activity limitation is based primarily upon qualified possession compensation incurred and depreciable assets employed, taxpayers should also reconsider a possession location for the production of more labor-intensive products. If there are products, product lines, or processes that are comparatively more labor-intensive, consideration should be given as to whether these products, product lines or processes may be more cost-effectively performed by the possession corporation.

Commentary 3: The changes to the possession credit alters the investment picture and requires a re-evaluation of alternative manufacturing incentives and locations. Companies that utilize profitable intangibles that will not benefit from the wage-based tax credit should consider other tax planning alternatives for future or current operations, such as transferring their possessions operations to a country with tax incentives for manufacturing. Many U.S. and foreign tax issues should be considered before implementing any alternative, including the new anti-deferral rules of §956A and the impact of transfer pricing rules on the use of intangibles needed for manufacturing or marketing activities.

Earnings Stripping and Other Anti-Avoidance Rules

EARNINGS STRIPPING RULES

◆ Prior Law

Under current law, there is a limit to the amount of interest expense that a foreign-owned U.S. subsidiary or branch of a foreign corporation may claim (the so-called *earnings stripping* rule). The earnings stripping rules apply to a corporation if it has a debt-to-equity ratio in excess of 1.5 to 1. In the case of such a corporation, interest paid to a foreign related tax-exempt person will be disallowed to the extent that such interest exceeds 50% of the corporation's adjusted taxable income for the year. Disallowed interest expense may be carried forward indefinitely and deducted in a tax year in which the corporation has *excess limitation* (i.e., net interest expense in an amount less than 50% of its adjusted taxable income). Legislative history indicates that regulations would clarify when a guarantee of third-party debt by a related tax-exempt person would constitute related-party debt.

◆ New Law

Interest paid on a loan from an unrelated party will be treated as disqualified interest if no gross basis U.S. income tax is imposed on the interest, a related person has guaranteed the loan, and the related person is either exempt from U.S. federal income tax or is a foreign person.

Except as provided in regulations, a guarantee would be defined to include any arrangement under which a person directly or indirectly assures (on an unconditional or contingent basis) the payment of another's obligation. For purposes of determining whether the interest paid on the guaranteed debt is exempt from United States tax, the fact that the unrelated lender is itself subject to net basis United States taxation (as opposed to United States withholding tax) on its interest income would not be taken into account. Regulations may also remove a guaranteed loan from the earnings stripping limitations if the interest would have been subject to net basis taxation if paid to the guarantor. If the taxpayer owns an 80% or greater interest in the guarantor, the interest would not be subject to limitation.

The earnings stripping rules would also apply to interest on any indebtedness issued on or before July 10, 1989 (or issued after such date pursuant to a binding written contract in effect on such date), notwithstanding that such debt was grandfathered by the original legislation.

Effective Date

The Act applies to any interest paid or accrued in tax years commencing after December 31, 1993.

> *Commentary:* The provision will significantly limit the opportunity to avoid the earnings stripping rules by using third party loans with related-party credit enhancements. Therefore, taxpayers may wish to begin negotiations with their banks to determine whether guarantees can be removed from existing debt. Without removing the guarantee, taxpayers wishing to avoid the earnings stripping limitations would need to ensure that their debt-equity ratio is less than 1.5 to 1, or that sufficient adjusted taxable income will be earned.

Strict Rules on Conduit Arrangements

The Treasury Department is authorized to issue potentially broad-ranging regulations that set forth rules (applicable to any section of the Code) for recharacterizing multiple-party financing arrangements as a conduit arrangement. The regulations would apply not only to back-to-back loans, but also to other financing transactions that in substance constitute a conduit arrangement.

Portfolio Debt Rules

The Internal Revenue Code is amended to provide that, except as provided in regulations, the portfolio interest exemption shall not apply to certain contingent interest paid to a nonresident alien or foreign corporation. The provision would apply to interest that is computed (directly or indirectly) on the basis of (1) gross or net income or cash flow (or any portion thereof, including income or cash flow derived from a particular property or a particular transaction) that is received or accrued by the debtor or a related person, or (2) the fair market value of property owned by the debtor or a related person (or the gain that would be realized from a disposition of such property). The provision would not override existing U.S. income tax treaties that reduce or eliminate U.S. withholding tax on interest paid to foreign persons.

Effective Date

The provision applies to interest paid or accrued on debt obligations issued after April 7, 1993.

> *Commentary:* The *Conference Report* indicates that, if a note contains a partial contingency,

only the amount which is contingent would not qualify for the portfolio debt.

EXAMPLE: Foreign Corp. A lends $100 to U.S. Corp. B. The interest is stated as the greater of 6% of the loan or 15% of gross profits. The amount of interest not allowed under the portfolio debt exemption, and therefore subject to U.S. withholding tax, is the excess of 15% of gross profits (contingent portion) over the stated 6% interest. All loans should therefore contain a stated interest rate approximating the contingency so that only the excess will be disallowed. This will also be necessary for estate tax planning, because the portion of debt deemed not contingent will qualify as portfolio debt and therefore not constitute U.S. property for estate tax purposes.

FOREIGN TAX CREDIT FOR OIL MULTINATIONALS

◆ Prior Law

As mentioned, United States taxpayers may claim a foreign tax credit for foreign taxes paid. The foreign tax credit is limited to the taxpayer's United States tax liability on foreign source taxable income. The foreign tax credit limitation is computed separately for specified categories of income.

One of the separate limitation categories is the *passive* category. Although most income of a passive nature falls into this category, interest on bank deposits or on other temporary investments of working capital in connection with foreign oil and gas extraction income (FOGEI), foreign oil-related income (FORI), or shipping income is excluded from the passive category. The exception for interest on working capital does not apply to other industries.

There is a special additional limitation on the amount of foreign oil and gas extraction or oil-related taxes that may be considered creditable against the United States tax on FOGEI or FORI. Passive income related to FOGEI and FORI is included in the computation of these limitations. The inclusion of interest on working capital in these limitations increases the amount of the foreign tax credit that may be claimed against United States tax on such income.

◆ New Law

The new law would prevent the cross-crediting of foreign taxes on FOGEI, FORI, and shipping income by placing investment income related to these types of income in the passive category for foreign tax limitation purposes. In addition, the law would exclude passive income from the definition of FOGEI or FORI for the computation of the FOGEI or FORI limitation on creditable taxes.

Effective Date

Tax years beginning after December 31, 1992.

> *Commentary:* Because passive earnings on working capital will no longer be beneficial in determining the foreign tax credit limitation related to FOGEI and FORI, companies in these industries should reevaluate the capital structure (and the required amount of working capital) of foreign affiliates.

7

◆ ◆ ◆ ◆ ◆ ◆ ◆

ENERGY TAXES

TRANSPORTATION FUELS TAX

◆ Prior Law

Multiple, separate, Federal excise taxes are imposed on certain transportation fuels, including the following: motor fuels used for highway transportation, gasoline used in motorboats, diesel fuel used in trains, fuels used in inland waterways transportation, and aviation fuel. The revenues from most of these excise taxes are dedicated to trust funds which finance different Federal public works projects and environmental programs.

One of the trust funds financed by an excise tax is the Leaking Underground Storage Tank ("LUST") Trust Fund, which is used to fund cleanup costs associated with leaking underground petroleum products storage. This 0.1 cent per gallon excise tax is imposed on all the fuel categories listed above. However, certain fuel uses are exempt from the LUST tax: gasoline and diesel fuel used on farms for farming purposes, off highway business uses (for example, fuel used to operate pumps, forklifts, trucks, or bulldozers, etc.), fuels used by State and local governments, fuels used by nonprofit educational organizations and fuel for military ships and aircraft.

◆ New Law

The Act imposes an additional new permanent transportation fuels excise tax of 4.3 cents per gallon on all transportation fuels currently subject to the LUST excise tax. In addition to the fuels subject to the LUST tax, the new transportation fuels tax would also be imposed on compressed natural gas used in highway motor vehicles or motorboats, and jet fuel used in noncommercial aviation. Gasoline and jet fuel used in commercial aviation received a two-year exemption from the tax but will be subject to it beginning on October 1, 1995.

The estimated effect of the 4.3 cents per gallon tax will be approximately $28.00 per year for the typical automobile driver and will generally be collected on removal of these fuels from registered terminal facilities.

The proceeds from the new tax are earmarked for deficit reduction and the revenue raised will be returned to the General Fund of the Treasury.

Effective Date

October 1, 1993. Floor stocks taxes will be collected on taxable fuels held for nonexempt activities on October 1, 1993.

COLLECTION OF DIESEL FUEL EXCISE TAX

◆ Prior Law

In general, taxes totaling 20.1 cents per gallon are imposed on the sale of diesel fuel by a producer or importer, with certain exemptions and reductions to the tax. These taxes are generally collected at the wholesale distributor level from the producer who makes the sale. Exempt and reduced-rate users who buy diesel fuel after the tax has been paid may file a claim for credit or refund, providing the proper business records are available for verification.

◆ New Law

The Act advances the point of collection of the full 20.1 cents per gallon diesel fuel excise tax to the time at which the gasoline is removed by truck from a terminal rack. Removal of fuel that is destined for an exempt use will not be taxed upon removal from the terminal so long as certain requirements to be established by the Treasury Department are met.

Effective Date

Diesel fuel removed from terminals on or after January 1, 1994. Note that an additional floor stocks tax is imposed on diesel fuel held beyond the terminal rack on this date.

> *Commentary:* Advancing the collection point of the diesel fuel taxes will reduce the number of times the fuel changes ownership prior to tax, as well as reduce the number of taxpayers. Therefore, the tax will be easier to collect and there will be less potential for evasion. Additionally, the burden placed upon exempt users of diesel fuel will be minimized.

EXTENSION OF MOTOR FUELS EXCISE TAX

◆ Prior Law

A portion of the excise taxes on motor fuels (gasoline, special motor fuels, and diesel fuel) is a 2.5 cents per gallon tax earmarked for deficit reduction and held in the General Fund of the Treasury. The tax does not apply after September 30, 1995.

◆ New Law

The Act extends the 2.5 cents per gallon tax on motor fuels through September, 1999. Further, the revenues from the tax that are collected from highway-related motor fuels will be dedicated to the Highway Trust Fund in order to meet the country's infrastructure needs. The revenues derived from non-highway fuels will remain in the General Fund, and the tax on diesel used in trains is 1.25 cents per gallon.

Effective Date

The extension applies after September 30, 1995.

IMPOSITION OF EXCISE TAX ON DIESEL FUEL USED IN NONCOMMERCIAL MOTORBOATS

◆ Prior Law

Although there are currently a number of Federal excise taxes imposed on diesel fuel used in land transportation vehicles, diesel fuel used in motor-boats is not currently taxed. The tax for diesel fuel used in highway transportation is currently 20 cents per gallon plus 0.1 cents per gallon to finance the Leaking Underground Storage Trust Fund (LUST).

◆ New Law

The Act imposes the current 20.1 cents per gallon taxes imposed on diesel used for highway transportation also on diesel fuel used in noncommercial motorboats. In addition, diesel fuel used by non-commercial motorboats also is subject to the new 4.3 cents per gallon transportation fuels tax. The tax on diesel fuel used by noncommercial motorboats will be collected at the same point as the tax on highway diesel fuels.

Effective Date

The imposition of these taxes on diesel fuel used in noncommercial motorboats will be effective after December 31, 1993.

8

◆ ◆ ◆ ◆ ◆ ◆ ◆

COMPLIANCE

EXPANSION OF 45-DAY INTEREST-FREE PERIOD FOR REFUNDS

◆ Prior Law

The IRS does not pay interest on a refund arising from an income tax return if the refund is issued by the later of: (1) the 45th day after the due date of the return (determined without regard to any extensions) or; (2) the date the return was filed. No such rule applies for refunds of taxes other than income taxes (e.g., employment taxes, excise taxes), for refunds of any type of tax arising from amended returns, or for claims for refunds of any type of tax.

◆ New Law

Under the Act, the 45-day interest-free period is extended to a refund arising from any type of original tax return. A parallel rule applies to amended returns and claims for refunds, and to IRS-initiated adjustments (e.g., computational adjustments or audit adjustments).

With respect to amended returns and claims for refunds, no interest will be paid by the government for the period of up to 45 days after the date the amended return or claim for refund is filed. However, interest will continue to be paid from the original due date to the date the amended return or claim for refund was filed. If the IRS does not issue the refund by the 45th day after the date the amended return or claim for refund is filed, interest will be paid from the due date of the original return to the date of payment of the refund. With respect to IRS-initiated adjustments, the government will pay interest for 45 fewer days than it otherwise would.

Effective Date

The extension of the 45-day processing rule is effective for returns required to be filed (without regard to extensions) on or after January 1, 1994. The amended return rule is effective for such returns or claims for refunds filed on or after January 1, 1995 (regardless of the taxable period to which they relate). The provision for IRS-initiated adjustments is effective for refunds paid on or after January 1, 1995 (regardless of the taxable period to which such refunds relate).

Commentary: This provision is designed to eliminate any reference to the type of tax involved for purposes of paying interest on tax refunds and, in effect, uniformily treats all types of federal taxes. Also, the modification of the interest rules with respect to amended returns and claims for refunds causes taxpayers to lose up to 45 days of interest on refunds issued within 45 days after the amended return or claim for refund is filed.

INFORMATION REPORTING (DISCHARGE OF INDEBTEDNESS)

◆ Prior Law

Generally, a taxpayer's gross income includes income from the discharge of indebtedness. Current law, however, does not require private lenders to file information returns with respect to discharge of indebtedness income. Treasury Department guidelines do require Federal agencies to report to the IRS forgiven debt amounts exceeding $600, except where prohibited by law. However, the Federal Deposit Insurance Corporation (FDIC) and the Resolution Trust Corporation (RTC) currently do not issue such reports because of concerns over violating the Right to Financial Privacy Act of 1978.

◆ New Law

Under the Act, *applicable financial entities* must file information returns with the IRS regarding any discharge of indebtedness of $600 or more. The same information must be provided to the person whose debt is discharged by January 31 of the year following the discharge.

Applicable financial entities include: (1) banks, trust companies, mutual savings banks, cooperative banks, savings institutions and credit unions; (2) the FDIC, the RTC, the National Credit Union Administration and any other Federal executive agency or sub-unit or successor thereof; and (3) any other corporation which is a direct or indirect subsidiary of an entity referred to above if it is subject to supervision and examination by a Federal or State agency which regulates such entities.

The penalties for failure to file correct information returns with the IRS and to furnish statements to taxpayers are similar to the penalties for failing to provide other information returns. For example, a $50 penalty per failure to furnish statements to taxpayers could apply up to a maximum of $100,000. The penalties do not apply if the failure was due to reasonable cause and not to willful neglect.

Effective Date

For non-governmental applicable financial entities, the new reporting requirements apply to discharges of indebtedness after December 31, 1993. In the case of government entities, the new rules apply to discharge of indebtedness after August 10, 1993.

Commentary: This provision is designed to place the FDIC and the RTC on an equal footing with other Federal agencies with respect to information reporting requirements for the discharge of indebtedness. Also, banks, trust companies and other *applicable financial entities* will be required to file information returns on any discharge of indebtedness in excess of $600 occurring after 1993. This increased information reporting requirement is aimed at aiding IRS enforcement of the discharge of indebtedness rules. Note that the definition of *applicable financial entities* excludes certain lenders, such as insurance companies and finance companies. Thus, covered entities will face information reporting compliance burdens not faced by other commercial lenders.

The new reporting requirements do not apply until the debtor is relieved of the liability. Therefore, charging off a debt or creating a reserve for its worthlessness will not have to be reported if the debtor continues to be liable for the debt.

INCREASED STANDARD FOR ACCURACY-RELATED AND PREPARER PENALTIES

◆ Prior Law

A 20% penalty is imposed on any portion of an underpayment of tax that is attributable either to a *substantial understatement* of income tax or to negligence or disregard of rules and regulations. A substantial understatement is one that exceeds the greater of 10% of the required tax or $5,000 ($10,000 for corporations other than S corporations and personal holding companies). *Negligence* generally includes any failure to make a reasonable attempt to comply with the internal revenue laws or to exercise ordinary and reasonable care in preparing a tax return, and *disregard* generally includes any careless, reckless, or intentional disregard of rules or regulations.

These penalties may be avoided by taxpayers where there has been adequate disclosure on the tax return and the position taken is not frivolous. A *frivolous* position for these purposes is one that is patently improper.

◆ New Law

Under the Act, the *not frivolous* standard has been replaced with the significantly more restrictive *reasonable basis* standard for purposes of the accuracy-related penalty. This standard cannot be satisfied by a return position that is merely arguable or a claim that is colorable. Instead, a position must have a *reasonable basis* before the substantial understatement penalty and the disregard of rules and regulations penalty may be avoided by adequate disclosure of the position. The disclosure exception for the negligence penalty is no longer applicable because a taxpayer generally is not considered to be negligent with respect to a return position that has a reasonable basis, regardless of disclosure.

Effective Date

The new provision is effective for tax returns due (without regard to extensions) after December 31, 1993.

> *Commentary:* This new law imposes a tougher standard on *taxpayers* when taking aggressive return positions. Thus, aggressive positions that are being considered for returns due on or after December 31, 1993, should be reviewed under the new *reasonable basis* standard. It should be noted that the *not frivolous* standard still applies to tax return *preparer* penalties.

The new law does not provide much assistance in determining when a *reasonable basis* for a position exists, with the legislative history stating only that such authority is present where it is *significantly higher* than that which satisfied the old *not frivolous* standard. In light of the new law, it would be advisable to give particular attention to positions that, under prior law, were merely arguable or colorable.

9

◆ ◆ ◆ ◆ ◆ ◆ ◆

MISCELLANEOUS ITEMS

The Act also includes a number of other significant provisions.

Increase Amount of Presidential Election Campaign Check-off. Effective for tax returns filed after 1993, the tax return checkoff for contributions to the Presidential Campaign Fund will increase from $1 to $3 for taxpayers who elect to earmark such amounts.

Orphan Drug Tax Credit. The tax credit for the clinical testing costs incurred to develop drugs for the treatment of rare diseases or physical conditions has been retroactively reinstated to its July 1, 1992 lapse and extended through the end of 1994.

Qualified Small Issue Bonds. The authority of local jurisdictions to issue tax-exempt bonds to finance the purchase or rehabilitation of owner-occupied homes, which lapsed July 1, 1992, has been retroactively reinstated and extended permanently.

Exports of Unprocessed Timber. The Act provides that any income from the sale of unprocessed timber which is a softwood and cut from an area within the U.S. would be categorized as domestic income. Other tax code provisions would also be amended to cut back on any tax subsidy for the export of such timber.

◆ ◆ ◆ ◆ ◆ ◆ ◆

INDEX

A

Accumulated earnings tax (AET), 55–56

Accumulated taxable income, 56

Adjusted current earnings (ACE), 61, 62

Adjusted gross income (AGI), and rule of limitation, 26, 27

Advance Pricing Agreement (APA), 167

Alternative minimum tax (AMT):
corporate, 55, 61–62
FSLIC assistance, 130
gifts of appreciated property, 32–35
individuals, 28–32

Alternative minimum taxable income (AMTI), 61–62

Amortization, intangible assets, 89–99

Anti-churning rule, 96–99

Arkansas Best issue, 128

B

Bankruptcy, and COD income, 100–102

Bonuses, 79–80

Business meals and entertainment, 65–66

C

C corporations:
and accumulated earnings tax (AET), 55–56
passive activity loss, 145–147
and personal holding company (PHC) tax, 56

Cancellation of indebtedness (COD) income:
and insolvency, 100
stock-for-debt exception, 100–102
tax attribute reductions, 103
title 11 bankruptcy, 100–103

Capital gains:
conversion transactions, 132–134
definition of investment income, 137–138
long term, 10
ordinary income *vs.*, 9–10
and Qualified Small Business Stock (QSBS), 46–47

Charitable contributions:
AMT exemption, 32–35
substantiation requirements, 35–38

Children:
and earned income tax credit (EITC), 19–20
and income shifting, 6

Club dues, 68–69

COD income, *see* Cancellation of indebtedness (COD) income

Community development corporations (CDCs), 88–89

Compensation:
  executive, 117–120
  retirement plan, 113–116

Conduit arrangements, 184–185

Controlled foreign corporations (CFCs), 171–178

Conversion transactions, 10
  criteria for, 132

Corporate estimated taxes:
  annualization of income, 57–59
  installment rate, 58

Corporate tax:
  possession-based operations, 178–182
  transfer pricing compliance, 164–168
  underpayment penalties, 53, 57

Corporate tax rates:
  alternative minimum tax (AMT), 55
  alternative minimum tax (AMT) relief, 61–62
  determination of annualized income, 58–60
  Financial Accounting Standard (FAS) 109, Accounting for Income Taxes, 53–55
  increase in rate, 50–55
  state and local, 106–109

D

Debt-financed real property, 150

Deductions:
  business meals and entertainment, 65–66
  club dues, 68–69
  intangible assets, 89–99
  itemized, reduction of, 14–16
  lobbying expenses, 70–73
  moving expenses, 63–65
  rental real estate losses, 144–148
  small business equipment (§179 property), 78–79
  travel expenses, spouses, dependents, and other individuals, 74–76

Deferral plans, 9

Depreciation:
  nonresidential real property, 162–163
  small business equipment, 78–79

Depreciation recapture, 156–157

Diesel fuel excise tax, 191–192
  extension of, 192–193
  imposition on noncommercial motorboats, 193–194

Discharge of Indebtedness:
  information reporting, 197–199
  real estate indebtedness, 153–158

E

Earned income tax credit (EITC), 19–23

requirements to qualify, 20–22

Earnings stripping rule, 182–186

Economic effects:
  budget deficit, xxxi–xxxvi
  economic growth and jobs, xl–xli
  energy conservation, xl
  productivity growth, xxxix
  short- and long-term interest rates, xxxvi–xxxvii

Educational assistance program, 110–112

Effective dates, xlii–xlvi

Employee:
  educational assistance programs, 110–112
  retirement plan compensation, 113–116
  travel expenses of spouses, 74–76

Employer, retirement plan deductible contribution, 113–116

Empowerment zones and Community Development Corporations (CDCs), 88–89
  enterprise communities, 80–89
  eligibility criteria, 81–83
  equipment expenditure write-off rule, 84
  Native American reservations, 86–87
  state incentive, 109
  tax benefits, 81–85
  tax-exempt bonds, 84–85
  wage credit, 83–84, 87

Energy tax:
  collection of diesel fuels, 191–192

extension of motor fuels, 192–193
  motorboats, 193–194
  transportation fuels, 189–190

Equipment expense, enterprise zone business, 84

Equipment expense, small business, 78–79

Estate tax, *see* Trusts and estates

Estimated tax:
  individual, 25–28
  corporate, 57–60

Excise tax, transportation fuels, 189–190

Exemptions, personal, 12–14

Exports of unprocessed timber, 202–203

F

Fixed-base percentage, start-up company, 76–78

Fixed-base period, 76

Foreign corporations:
  conduit arrangements, 184–185
  earnings stripping rule, 182–186
  investment in U.S. property, 177–178
  Subpart F income, 176

Foreign earnings, tax deferral, 170–175

Foreign oil and gas extraction income (FOGEI), 186–188

Foreign oil related income (FORI), 186–188

401(k) plans, 9, 116

Franchise amortization, 99

FSLIC assistance, 129–131

and bad debt, 130
  effective dates, 130–131

G
Gift tax rates, 38–40
Goodwill, *see* Intangible assets

H
Health insurance, deductions
  for the self-employed,
  42–43

I
Incentive stock options
  (ISOs), 10
Income tax brackets, 1–4
Indexing, 4, 13, 113, 114
Individual tax rates, 1–4
Information reporting,
  discharge of indebtedness,
  197–199
Installment payments, 4
Intangible assets:
  anti-churning rule, 96–99
  created *vs.* acquired, 89–90
  criteria for amortization, 90–
    91
  exclusions from amortiza-
    tion, 92–93
  loss deferral rule, 93–95
  property acquisition, 96
Intangible property, binding
  contract election, 96
Itemized deductions, 14–16
Interest-free refunds, 195–197
Investment income, described, 137
Investments, tax-exempt, 7–8
IRAs, 9

J
Joint filing, 6

K
Kiddie tax, 6, 12
Keogh plans, 9

L
Large corporation, for purpose
  of estimated taxes, 57
Leaking Underground Storage
  Tank ("LUST") Trust Fund,
  189, 193
Life insurance, 9
Lobbying expense, disallowance
  rules, 70–73
Long-term capital gains, 10, 43
Loss deferral rule, 93–95
Low-income housing credit,
  141–142
Luxury excise tax, 40–42

M
Market discount rules, 134–135
Mark to market rules, 121–128
Marriage penalty tax, 6–7
  and divorce, 6–7
  and wedding date, 6
Meals and entertainment
  expenses, deductions, 65–66
Medicare:
  accelerating income, 25
  tax increase, 23
Modified accelerated cost
  recovery system (MACRS),
  61, 62
Mortgage revenue bonds, 142–
  143
Moving expenses, deduction,
  qualifications, 63–65

N
Native American business tax
  incentives, 86–87

Nonqualified stock options (NSOs), 10
Nonrecognition transactions, under intangibles, provisions, 95

O

Ordinary income, *vs.* capital gains, 9–10
Original issue discount (OID), 135–136
Orphan drug tax credit, 202
Overtime, 79–80

P

Partnerships:
    real property indebtedness, 157
    redemptions, 158–161
    substantially appreciated inventory, 138–139
Pass-through entities, 46
Passive activity:
    cancellation of indebtedness, 102–106
    deduction eligibility, 143–147
    described, 143–144
Passive foreign investment asset test, 174
    corporation (PFIC), 171–175
Penalties, 198–201
    accuracy-related, 199–201
    corporate, underpayment of estimated taxes, 53
    transfer pricing, 164–168
Performance-based compensation, 118–120
Personal exemptions, 12–14
Personal holding company (PHC), 56

Portfolio debt rules, 185
Possession corporations, 178
Presidential campaign check-off, 202
Property acquisition, intangible assets, 96
Property:
    depreciation of nonresidential real estate, 162–163
    partnership redemptions, 158–161
Property expensing:
    Native American business investment, 86
    small business, 78–79

Q

QSBS, see Qualified small business stock (QSBS)
Qualified mortgage bonds (QMBs), 142–143
Qualified possession source investment income (QPSSI), 178–179
Qualified real property business indebtedness:
    defined, 154
    limitations, 155
Qualified retirement plan, 113–116
Qualified small business stock (QSBS), exclusion, 44–48
Qualified small issue bonds, 202

R

Rate levels, 3–4
Real estate:
    passive activity loss, 144–148
    and pension funds, 149–153
Real estate investment trust (REIT), 149–153

Real property:
  debt-financed, 149–153
  depreciation of nonresidential, 162–163
  discharge of indebtedness, 153–158
  trade or business, described, 147
Refunds, interest-free, 195–197
Rental real estate, passive activity loss, 143–148
Research credit, 76–78
  expense allocation rules, 168
  extension, 75
  start-up companies, 75
Restaurants:
  employee tip income, 65
Retirement plans, 113–116
Rev. Proc. 92–56, 169, 170

S
S Corporation, real property indebtedness, 157
Safe harbor rule, estimated taxes, 57
Securities, 121–128
Securities dealers, mark to market method, 122
Small business:
  equipment expense, 78–79
  and qualified small business stock (QSBS), 44–48
Social Security benefits, taxation of, 16–19
Specialized small business investment company (SSBIC), 48, 49–50
SSBIC, *see* Specialized small business investment company
State tax liability, and federal law, 106–109
Stock-for-debt exception, 100–102
Stripped preferred stock, 135–136
Subpart F income, 171–172, 176
Substantially appreciated inventory, 138–139
Supplemental wage payments, 79–80
Surtax, high-income individuals, 1

T
Targeted jobs tax credit, 112–113
Tax credits:
  community development corporations contributions, 87–88
  earned income tax credit, 19–23
  employer, for FICA taxes on tip income, 66–68
  enterprise zone business, 83–84
  foreign oil, 186–188
  low-income housing, 141–142
  Native American business incentives, 86–87
  orphan drug credit, 202
  possession-based operations, 178–182
  research and development, 76–78
  targeted jobs, 112–113
  enterprise zone business, 84–85
Tax-exempt investments, 7–8
  trusts and estates, 12

Tax rates, 4–6,
  individual, 12–14
  capital gains, 131–132
  corporate, 51–53
  supplemental wages, 79–80
  trusts and estates, 11–13
Tip income, 66–68
Trademark/tradename
  amortization, 99
Transfer pricing, 164–168
Travel expenses, spouses,
  dependents and other
  individuals, 74–76
Trusts and estates:
  income spreading, 12

  tax rates, 11–13

U
Unrelated business taxable
  income (UBTI), 149–153

W
Wages:
  Native American business
    credits, 86–87
  employer wage, 83–84
Withholding rate on
  supplemental wages:
  bonuses, 79–80
  commissions, 79–80